M000107725

# GENERATION WE SOLVE

## Cause the Effect

# GENERATION WE SOLVE

## Cause the Effect

Joshua Murphy

© 2011 by Joshua Murphy

All rights reserved. No part of this book may be reproduced, stored in a retrieval system, or transmitted in any form or by any means without the prior written permission of the publishers, except by a reviewer who may quote brief passages in a review to be printed in a newspaper, magazine, or journal.

First Printing

ISBN-13: 978-0615478661

*This book is dedicated to my family and all those who seek to create positive social change.*
FDM 1937-2009

# Acknowledgments

Thanks to my parents Velma and Franklin for always believing in me and supporting all of my creative adventures. To my family for their support and love over the years. To my friends for encouraging my creative sparks. To my many church families for their love and support. To my fraternity Sigma Phi Epsilon for truly inspiring me to reach for a life with purpose and sacrifice. To Marissa McCauley for assisting with editing the book and Renee Gerstein for her awesome book cover design. And to Zach Schultz for his studious help in many creative aspects of this book.

This book is dedicated to all those who strive for a life worth living and a life filled with idealism and purpose.

Please visit my website at: http://www.thejoshmurphy.com

**Credits:**

3-d model created by Veronica.
Map created from DEMIS Mapserver, public domain, licensed under the Creative Commons Attribution-Share Alike 3.0 Unported license:
**http://creativecommons.org/licenses/by-sa/3.0/deed.en**

# Contents

PREFACE ...................................................................................... 1

INTRODUCTION ...................................................................... 5

1. FAILING A GENERATION ............................................... 13

2. HAVE FAITH IN YOURSELF .......................................... 45

3. LIVING WITH A PURPOSE AND MAKING A PLAN ....... 67

4. PLANTING A SEED AND CHANGING THE WORLD ........ 91

5. FINDING YOURSELF, BY GIVING OF YOURSELF .......... 113

6. SEEKING A LOST GENERATION .................................... 123

ABOUT THE AUTHOR ................................................... 167

# PREFACE
## SOCIAL CHANGE THROUGH IDEAS AND ACTIONS

Writing for me is about spreading ideas that cause one to pause, and to put themselves in another person's shoes to reevaluate their own life and how they plan to leverage their talents to change the world for the better. Since I was about nine years old, I have been moved by the power of words and the emotions words can create by igniting the spirit within. I always found myself writing short stories and spending countless hours in the local public library reading anything I could grasp my hands on from Curious George to Dr. Seuss to entrepreneurial books. Growing up in a small town there was not much to do, so for me building up my imagination through the power of reading was my true happiness. And once I began to feel such inspiration from those words, the next logical step was to create my own writings.

The realization of my gift began simply from the letters I wrote to President Clinton on education reform and school violence, and to my favorite authors requesting autographs and praising their work, which then grew into creating my own stories.

Within those stories politics and social advocacy seemed to be the main focus of my writings. I was constantly researching and learning about issues I felt impacted the lives of people my age: education, violence, poverty, disease, and community development. I wrote for my school newspapers and even found it exciting to write business plans. By the time I entered high school I was fully enthralled by the power of words and how they could impact others to act.

I became close friends with the local editor of my town's newspaper and began writing my own political column on issues affecting not just our community, but our nation and world. And within each of those writings I always attempted to not just discuss the issues, but to come up with plausible solutions. During my senior year of high school, I had amassed so many writings and columns I decided to publish my first book, *Writings from a Teenage Mind*. This was my first entry into the publishing world and for me it was always about spreading my ideas, in hopes that others would be inspired to seek their own gifts and to express them. While in college, I continued to hone my writing skills through my blog which I utilized like my own personal writing space.

My blog to this day is a place I express my thoughts, emotions, beliefs, and ideas on how we all have not just a right, but a responsibility to make the world a better place for future generations. I have always believed in the power of community and the responsibility that entails, that we are our brothers' and sisters' keeper, and that this world cannot exist unless we each realize and embrace that responsibility, not merely as a burden, but as an opportunity. This is an opportunity to inspire, to create, to build, and not just to take from, or to use, and abuse. Life is such a precious gift; it comes and goes in the blink of an eye.

I always question myself and what I can do to positively impact the world aside from just volunteering or donating to a social cause. It truly is a great feeling when we make someone smile, help an elderly person rebuild their porch or give to a non-profit group to support impoverished nations. However, I always feel as though my work is left undone, that together we can do much more. *Generation We Solve: Cause the Effect* is the beginning of that life journey to create lasting opportunity and to instill lifelong values and ideals into the hearts and minds of my peers that will cause our nation and the world to embrace social change and most importantly, to be an instigator and creator of innovation and creativity.

The idea that the talents and gifts of one individual can be transformed and transferred to another is an inspiring thought. Not merely for a moment, but for a generation. The problems we face in America and the world are great—from climate change to poverty to eradicating diseases to providing clean drinking water in third world countries to reforming education so it works not just for a few, but for all to bringing civility back into our global discourse. I would hate to think that when my time on this earth comes to a close, when the light dimmers, I had been standing on the sidelines as a spectator, instead of as an involved, dedicated, and forceful agent for change.

*Generation We Solve: Cause the Effect* is my challenge to not only myself, but to the world to rise above the divisive, the hateful, the spiteful, the disengaged, and the hopeless into a realm of openness, development, idealism, purpose, and opportunity. This is not a stroll, this is a lifelong journey to discover, embrace, and impart a sense of hope and purpose upon those who are willing to fight the good fight for the sake of humanity. Let us all put petty differences aside to think for a moment about how we can be united, how we can all be a force for positive and sustainable social change.

I have always believed in the power of the individual to enact sustainable social change, which is the ability to transform the world in which we live structurally, socially, and economically to benefit others who are pulling and grasping for life, so they too can become active participants in society. The power of WE is the cornerstone of humanity and its future, not just I. It is my belief that each and every person has a special gift that is to be used to empower others and to make a difference in the lives of others. The world is a very challenging environment—the bumps and bruises we endure on the journey of life prepare us for the success ahead, what many call the light at the end of the tunnel.

The pulling and grasping for something that is greater than us, the determination to impact the world, to leave a legacy and to know that our efforts are not in vain is the promise of an enduring humanity. This humanity can only be if we strive for it, if we fight for it, if we believe in it—the wholeness of life, the fulfillment of a destiny is only achieved if we seek it. Words are powerful, ideas are powerful, but what is truly powerful is when those words and ideas are put into action. And then that action causes another reaction—it begins to flow like an autumn rain, that moment in which we realize that our destiny is upon us. We realize that we are not merely an idea or voice in the wind, we are alive. We no longer accept the status quo, barriers are broken, and walls are torn down. The power within is finally unleashed and our God-given talents are fully embraced to make a positive difference in our lives and in our world.

Many people are afraid of the good inside of them and the endless possibilities that we all posses to change the world. My hope is that through my writings one will be inspired to live their innermost dreams and take the theoretical into the realm of practicality. I challenge you to discover your story, your purpose, and to not only embrace it but share it. In the words of Mahatma Gandhi, *"We must be the change we wish to see."*

# INTRODUCTION

As our society becomes more intertwined with the global community, we must continue to promote innovation and social sustainability. We must not only promote innovation and social sustainability abroad to foster freedom and independence, but also here at home. The premise of global success in the 21$^{st}$ Century must be a strong and vibrant America. In order to foster a positive global economic recovery, America must develop new energy resources, reduce our national debt, promote ethical scientific research, continue to lead in technological innovation, create an education system that realizes the challenges of our future, decrease the wealth gap through targeted economic and social development programs, and promote international development that opens doors for millions of impoverished and oppressed peoples. Through our own positive show of innovation and social sustainability we will show others across the world a nation dedicated to positive social change that is not only aimed at America, but the world at large.

Countries and citizens across the world view America as a beacon of hope and opportunity. They look to our nation to lead on multiple fronts. Therefore, we must engage our allies and those who support democracy, openness, and liberty in this multinational endeavor. To simply lay the burden and cost of promoting innovation and social sustainability to our nation would fail to recognize the interconnectedness of our global economy and society. The more ideas and opportunities available to people across the world to take control of their own lives, the more likely we can build an international system that relies not merely on the power and outreach of America, but each nation's own individual ingenuity and sustainability.

Working with individuals, corporations, non-governmental organizations, government agencies, and groups of all sorts, America can lead a new era of engagement and growth the world has never seen. The flow of information, technology, and the democratization of the Internet can play a pivotal role in our quest to spread democracy and liberty. Once people all across the world experience the positive impact of innovation and self-sustainability, they will see America's motives are peaceful and hopeful, both in nations who share our values of human rights and respect, and those who impede the freedom of human opportunity.

America in the 21st Century must not only depend on its military superiority to promote freedom and opportunity, but also focus on international development and economic growth. Through our ability to make a positive difference in developing nations to lift people out of poverty and dependence into self-sustainability and prolonged economic growth, we will have shown the ability of soft power to make a positive difference in the world. Our ability to connect and interact with people of different ideals, cultures, and beliefs will have not just positive short term outcomes, but also long-term effects.

America must continue to be a shining beacon of hope and prosperity for those who value freedom, justice, and opportunity. Building up developing nations and creating positive relationships that are built on trust and partnership is our calling in the 21st Century. The relationships we build today will guide future generations for years to come. Nations who seek to step out of a system of international norms and values should be isolated and made to realize that a world built on trust and positive interactions with their fellow neighbors is a system all nations should attain to.

## Science and Health Technology

America must also lead in scientific research once again. The H1N1 Virus showed our vulnerabilities in times of a global pandemic. Through our funding of government and university research we can once again create the medicines, vaccines, cures, and medical technologies of the future. We can also build partnerships with other nations to coordinate new scientific studies and advances. We must also seek to ensure research values safety, restraint, and evaluation to ensure all precautions are being taken to facilitate ethical medical research and product development. Travel and open borders throughout the world increases the likelihood of diseases spreading faster and more uniquely than ever before. Using health data, open lines of communication, and the newest advances in detection and treatment, the world can unite around the common cause of locating the source and eradicating old and new diseases before they grow to pandemic levels.

America must lead in the 21st Century in providing affordable and accessible health care to all of its citizens, reducing long-term health care costs for individuals, businesses and government, promoting preventive health care, and utilizing the advancements in medical technology to make America more competitive and healthy. Expanding health care to low-income communities in both rural and urban environments must be a top priority to improve health care access across America. By promoting wellness and exercise programs in schools and communities alike, we can once again lead in new and innovative health initiatives across the world. A healthy and prosperous community here at home can actively engage in a new and competitive global economy abroad.

## The Environment and Energy

Ensuring a healthy environment for future generations is one of the most monumental and important challenges of our time. Climate change poses a grave challenge to the world. We must protect our air, water, forests, wetlands, and landmarks from destruction. The realization that the beauty of this planet is one of our most sacred vows as a people that must be renewed and sustained is a solemn undertaking. America must lead the world in reducing greenhouses gases, promoting sustainable development, and creating new means of renewable energy technology. Through the renewal of our environment and the development of clean energy technology, America can lead the world into a cleaner future based on energy innovation.

We must work with our allies and developing countries such as India and China to develop an agreed-upon system of mutual interests that place environmental and energy conservation ahead of self-interests. Our choices today in dealing with the rejuvenation of our environment and our pursuit of clean energy technologies will determine whether or not we have a global economy built on the foundation of a prosperous environment for future generations or one that struggles to provide clean air, water, and land for economic development and human growth needs. We must all make tough choices in terms of balancing the need for robust economic growth and the sustainability of our planet.

America and nations all across the world must come together on this issue to ensure the survivability of all people on every corner of this earth. We are all inextricably linked on this issue—no matter if we live in New Delhi or New Hampshire, Hong Kong or Florida. As we continue to invest in clean energy, new modes of transportation, infrastructure, and innovative technologies today, we must always keep in mind our quest for a brighter, cleaner tomorrow.

## International Development

Fostering relationships with citizens all across the world is vital in the 21$^{st}$ Century. Empowering people to take control of their own communities and individual outcomes not only instills within them a sense of pride and achievement, but also helps create a more open and economically independent society. One of the most positive and influential ways America can make a positive and lasting difference in other nations is through economic and social development. By providing the tools, resources, knowledge, and training to citizens in developing nations; America can be a harbinger of economic and self-development all across the world. Building villages, schools, health centers, and providing access to business innovation will open new doors of freedom and sustainability for millions of people all across the world.

America can do more good in the world through international development than it can through war and destruction. By showing people that we care not only about their short term but also their long term prosperity, we create a new level of engagement and community service that will reap huge dividends in the years to come. Lifting people out of poverty and into economic self-sufficiency reduces the possibility of war, government dependence, and hopelessness. America has always been a shining example of freedom, liberty, and opportunity. The more we spread the values of our society to others, the more people of all nations will see that our intentions are grounded in a hope and promise that a stronger and more prosperous global community is not a threat to America, but a chance for us to unite to lift even more people out of the darkness of poverty and seclusion and into the light of innovation and social sustainability.

## Wealth and Economic Growth

In order for America to lead an even bolder international system, the nation must first improve its own economic and social policies aimed at bridging the great wealth divide between low and high-income Americans, improve its own economic output and growth, and reduce its national debt. Income stagnation in America is an issue that has not been fully addressed as it should be. Median incomes and those at the top of the economic ladder are deeply divided mostly due to unfair tax and government policies that favor those with higher incomes. Due to the recent recession, middle and low income families have suffered the most.

These families have endured a dramatic loss of funds due to joblessness, reductions in savings, investments, college funds, real estate, and the decline in the ability to live sustainable and prosperous lives. The declining wealth of middle and low-income families has increased the burden of government to step in as a social safety net for millions of families. However, long-term structured debt, tax structures, and entitlement programs pose an even greater challenge for American policy makers to improve the long-term economic growth of the country. America can once again empower a rejuvenation of economic growth for those struggling to stay afloat economically by investing in education, energy innovation, entrepreneurship, and a reformed tax code.

We must create policies and programs that empower and reward low and middle-income communities who create innovative businesses, save and invest, and reduce their debt—this will determine the future of America's middle class. American policy makers must continue to revive its manufacturing base, increase fair trade, promote ethical and sustainable business behavior, revive regulation to reduce unnecessary risk to the financial system, and bring leaders across business, government, and the non-profit world together to increase innovation and social sustainability within our economy in an ever changing global society. It is also vital for America to reduce its national debt.

This will require tough choices in the restructuring of entitlement programs, taxes, and spending (both discretionary and non-discretionary). However, leaders must keep in mind the sensitivity many communities and people are feeling all across the nation as the economy continues to recover from the Great Recession. America can be a shining example for the entire world in terms of creating long term economic growth that is fair and sustainable. Nation's all across the world depend on a prosperous and innovative America to spark ingenuity and economic growth for millions.

## Education

Our efforts to reform education today will have a direct effect on our nation's ability to respond to the challenges of the present and the future. America must build an education system that recognizes the increasing challenges in science, math, and technology innovation. Leaders must work together to revamp curriculum standards, standardized testing, teacher professional development, classroom structure, and individual student achievement to ensure we are measuring the correct outcomes and giving our young people the best opportunity to succeed and excel at the challenges of the 21st Century.

Education is one of the defining issues of our generation. We no longer face just economic challenges within our own states, but also across borders and oceans. Improving the educational outcomes for students in low-income rural and urban communities is an issue of equality and opportunity. Businesses expect a future workforce that values diversity, openness, idealism, and innovation. Our young people must be given the tools and resources that do not just meet expectations, but greatly exceed them. Holding students to minimal levels of learning is a recipe for disaster. They must be held to the highest standards of learning, evaluation, and opportunity. When America's students succeed, so does the rest of the world.

Those who attain degrees are economically more sufficient and independent. For those who seek to reduce government dependence and social programs should look no further than our education system as the solution. No child should be left in the dark and every child deserves at least the opportunity to live their dream. The education system must also hold teachers accountable through continued professional development, measurement, and accountability. Just as student success should not only be measured by standardized test, nor should teachers. Education leaders must use a multi-faceted approach in how they evaluate both teachers and students that is rooted in a diversity of opinions, measuring tools, and unbiased outcomes. Spreading educational opportunities here in America and abroad is one of the greatest and important challenges of our time. Providing people with the gift of an education is the key to innovation and social sustainability.

## Conclusion

Change is not easy, which is why America cannot fail. The world depends on a strong and prosperous United States that recognizes the challenges of today while developing solutions to the challenges of the future. America must lead in its quest to empower not only its own citizens, but citizens all across the world who value freedom, liberty, and justice. The challenges we face are monumental, therefore our solutions must meet those challenges with the same vigor and attitude as we have met every challenge since our founding. Renewing America's sense of national opportunity and hope, while at the same time leading the world in the 21st Century to a more open, safe, and prosperous future will require an altruistic foundation of support and innovation.

We must share solutions, ideas, and systems to solve the problems we all face in our current and future environments; building new technologies to promote cleaner energy and environmental conservation; developing a robust and cooperative health care system based on the newest technologies and innovations in both care and accountability; promoting an education system that prepares our young people for the global challenges of tomorrow; advocating for a system of economic renewal, opportunity, and sustainability for those with middle/low incomes; and developing new systems and outreach mechanisms to promote international development that builds sustainable communities. These are the challenges of our time. These are the opportunities that hold our own futures in our hands. Through America's partnerships with its allies and other freedom loving nations, the 21st Century can be a bold new adventure that realizes not our fears or failures, but our hopes and dreams.

# 1
# FAILING A GENERATION

*"Life is no brief candle to me. It is a sort of splendid torch which I have got a hold of for the moment, and I want to make it burn as brightly as possible before handing it onto future generations."*
— George Bernard Shaw

What exactly has gone wrong? Do young people today feel as though they are being heard? Why are their talents and ideals being blinded and left in the dark? How can we awaken a lost generation? These are many of the questions I will seek to answer in this section. There is much still to learn about Generation Y or Gen Y (those born from the mid-1970s to the early 2000s). If we do not awaken Gen Y and its compelling force to achieve greatness, we will continue to lose ground to other industrialized nations in education, technology, and innovation. We must teach our young people that each of them has a unique purpose, and we are here to guide them along their life path.

## How We Are Failing a Generation and What We Can Do to Change It

Education reform today seems to be entirely focused on measuring success via standardized testing, graduation rates, and teacher accountability. Of course these are all important—but the question still remains—are young people better off today to tackle the many challenges we face than past generations and even comparatively to other developed nations? The answer is NO. We have all seen the studies showing how our students measure up in math and science to other countries—not so good.

It cannot be due to a lack of testing and grading, because we do plenty of those things! Nor can it be because we are not trying hard enough to implement strategies to graduate students from high schools, because we are! Nor can it be because teachers are not being held accountable—because to be perfectly honest, it does not seem school systems in general are holding themselves accountable. The key link here that we are missing is the link between success in the classroom and the sense of empowerment, motivation, hope, purpose, and success our young people feel once they are in school and out of school.

Do our young people feel as though they have a purpose on this earth? If so, do they feel as though education in its current form is helping them reach their career and academic goals? Do young people feel as though adults listen to them? Do they feel as though their creativity and independence are being encouraged and cultivated in an active, clean, safe, and inspiring learning environment? Do young people today feel a sense of self-worth and self-motivation derived from a core belief that education in the 21$^{st}$ Century is a means for success not only in the present, but the future? Are we helping to mold our young people to truly utilize their gifts and talents? These talents are in the fields of music, art, sports, science, and a whole myriad of other possibilities and career interests. Are the voices of Generation Y being heard? Do we care? If so, what can we do to implement a new strategy for empowering and engaging a lost generation? We must, we can, and we will—for the sake of not only our nation's best interest, but for a better society on earth.

We have allowed our own judgment to be clouded by a national educational system in limbo that has never truly been re-calibrated to focus on the needs, ideals, and aspirations of Generation Y. We have to focus not just on the textbooks, the desks, the buildings, the teachers, and the standardized tests, but on the hearts and souls of our young people. We must not only engage the youth of today, but empower them—shock and awe—to realize that their future is in their hands—and we are all simply a very small, incremental part of that process—guides of sorts—they are the builders, the molders, thinkers, creators, designers, dancers, singers, athletes, and dreamers. We are here to listen, to assist, to mentor, to be a light for a brighter, clearer path in their quest for happiness, success, growth, and long-term stability and prosperity.

We can do this by:

A) Instituting constant communication between young people and adults.

B) Mentoring, guiding, and rehabilitating those students who are in need of the most help to succeed.

C) Constant motivation, positive thinking, and support to give our most disadvantaged youth hope for a brighter tomorrow.

D) Creating an education system that cultivates and mixes with the goals, visions, and ideals of our young people—that embraces diversity and independent growth.

E) Empathy training for those who work with our young people so they can be better listeners and guide our youth in positive directions.

F) Investing in creating a clean slate in the lives of young people—essentially starting over and giving them the opportunity to write their own destiny, their own future, and vision for life.

We can do this—we must, in order to create a more just, free, open, and prosperous society for today and for the future. Education reform is not just about a building or a book or a teacher, it is truly about the hearts and souls of young people—they need us now more than ever—we cannot leave them now—instead we must focus intently on engaging and empowering them to aim high, to never give up, and guide them through the trials and tribulations of life so that they too will become free, independent, idealistic, and successful individuals.

## Getting Education Back on Track in the 21st Century

As many states have now turned to standardized testing, American students, parents, and educators will once again be fooled into believing our school systems are improving and preparing students for this new society of globalization and information convergence. But in reality, students are once again getting the short end of the stick, and our education system is no better off today than it was 25 years ago. Students should be taught real world learning, with a deep focus on what they want to learn, how they learn, and what interest them education wise. Teaching today is pushing students to remember a mass amount of facts and numbers, rather than challenging students to better understand what this information means. We have to push our students today to think about what they are reading and learning, not to just do it and only think about making an exceptional grade.

If a student makes an A+ on everything he or she does, but yet fails to remember any of it and its real purpose, than no learning has occurred and we as a society have failed. If a student picked up a book and read it because he or she had to compared to a student who read a book because he or she wanted to, it is more likely that the student who wanted to read that book is actually going to think about what they read and have gained knowledge from it. Students today have so many distractions with the integration of media and technology. If our schools are not three steps ahead of the game there will continue to be a dramatic decline in the ability of students who actually want to learn compared to those who feel forced to attend class every day. It is pretty obvious that when a student is excited and interested in what they are learning, they are more likely to be engaged, in tune, and studious about the subject. They are going to ask questions, want to gain a deeper knowledge, and have a better and longer lasting understanding of the subject matter.

Students in today's society must be challenged to question everything, to try new experiments, generate new ideas, and be pioneers of learning in this new and exciting global learning environment. There is much more underneath the surface that is waiting for students all across America to discover and dig deeper, but standardized testing and this same old approach of teaching numbers, facts, and theories will continue to hinder students from realizing their true potential. Students must be given a chance to dream, create goals and visions, and map their own education. Educators and parents must be open to what students have to say about learning, what excites them and makes them want to attend classes and actually gain something from it. The government has wasted too much time legislating their way of teaching on schools and teachers.

There must be change and its times for parents, students, and local educators to take a real stand and fight for what they know is right and what works. Students deserve better, and they deserve to be heard loud and clear. School is not a business; it is a service to our children, to our country, and to our futures. The young men and women that come out of our schools should be excited about going farther in life and expanding their horizons of learning. Students must be taken seriously and given real control of their education now, rather than later. If we want our students to mature and grow to do great things in this world, we cannot continue to give them a broken system and the wrong way of doing things; we must open up our schools to a new way of thinking and learning, where students are heard and given a chance to learn.

There must be a constant and healthy dialogue between school officials, parents, students, and leaders. It is truly unfair how students are forced to learn the same way as past generations and are not given the chance to try new and exciting technologies and curriculums. And as a former public school student, I have heard these same complaints from students, parents, and teachers in the past. But yet students and families are being forced to accept these education policies that are wrong and unfair to our society. We can do better, and I challenge all stakeholders to fight for what they believe in and to never give up. Our nation's future hangs in the balance; therefore, we the people can no longer stand back and continue to watch our education system fall apart as it is today.

## The Moral and Ethical Basis for Sustainable Social Change

I would be a fool to simply believe that the mere acknowledgment of truth and the promise of social progress will within itself enact such change. Even with the work of past giants, leaders, and fighters—there is much to do. The struggles that we each face to reconcile our fear of change with our own innate understanding that life and liberty should not be a product for the few, but for all who seek it, is continuously ongoing. Our hearts seek such humility and humanity, such promise and peace, such hope and prosperity. However, we face on this earth an unlikely wind to the contrary. A wind that shifts with the trials and tribulations of our time—our own self vices and wants—not necessarily with our longing for something better, something greater than ourselves.

As the transgressions of past generations shall not be forgotten, nor should our own failures be forgotten, to actively create and promote the social change in which we seek here in the present. We watch in earnest and in desperation as our own human hands destroy our ecosystem. We see those we elect to lead simply squabble and bicker without resolution—deal and manipulate—rather than do the will of the people. A society that in the words of the late Martin Luther King Jr., *"prizes property rights over human rights,"* what must we do to realize the change we truly seek is right here before our eyes? Through our acknowledgment of failing to do more to right the wrongs of the past, to build a brighter future, and to finally reconcile the dreams of those past with the hopes of today, we can then realize that our hopes and ideals are not as far apart as we are led to believe.

I sincerely believe that by engaging in a continuous, open, and intelligent dialogue we can find common ground to society's social ills. With the advent of social media, technology, networking, and social entrepreneurship—we can actively imagine and create both the real social change we seek and that of which has been promoted for centuries and generations. I find that the optimism and truth of the human spirit always exceeds the hatred and negativity of present uncomfortable situations. We should not see economic opportunity and human dignity as an either-or-proposition. Nor should we view justice and equality as a detriment to individuality and economic freedom. Human progress and social progress should not be viewed as zero sum endeavors. Instead, the progression of human rights, social stability, innovation, and economic justice should be viewed as a means to empower people to become their own sustainable engines of economic growth and prosperity.

When people feel empowered, capable, educated, and connected to a social structure that values ethics, hard work, and freedom, they are simply more likely to succeed—not only in the mere terms of his or her own understandings and norms of success, but in societal terms. Each individual person has their own ideals, dreams, aspirations, and visions for their life. No one can take those away—but what a society can do is help to make those dreams and goals a reality. Every child has the potential to achieve their dreams—no border, race, belief, or economic background shall be the determinant of that child's future—this should be the guiding principle of a society that wishes to enact positive and sustainable social change. The belief that generational crutches—from a lack of wealth to a lack of education—should not determine the outcome of a future generation of young people must be the call of a society seeking to instill a principal of equal opportunity. Each society must decide where it stands—it must decide the values it will uphold, and it must honor those values continuously without regard to creed, color, or historical bias. The future success of a generation depends on its ability to recognize the creativity, idealism, and hope of those in the present and, through positive and sustainable social change, this noble goal can be achieved.

## Education Reform Can Occur: No Excuses, Just Results

I am always interested in different programs and schools of learning. I heard about Andre Agassi's College Preparatory Academy in Las Vegas on Oprah and was very inspired. Many people have given up on public education and specifically those schools in our inner city communities. We can improve our public schools and it is not all about money. It is about creating a culture of education and learning, in a time where many young people are swamped with technology and social media.

Education is by far the most powerful equalizer in our society. A young child born in a household with one parent can achieve ultimate success through a rigorous and comprehensive education that is not based on excuses, but results.

Our teachers, parents, and students alike must all be on the same page, and students must know what is expected from them as stewards of the future of our society. We all have a purpose and meaning on this earth and we are all responsible for ensuring that every child has a chance to succeed in life. We as a nation cannot afford to fail our students, no matter if they are born in the wealthiest neighborhood or the poorest.

Reaching out to young people, discovering their potential and talents in life is essential to developing a future education system that is not a one size fits all way of thinking, but one in which we provide a real commitment to individual attention, diversity, and technology to prepare our students for an even more challenging globalized economy and work place. This will not be easy by any stretch of the imagination, considering our public school system is still stuck in the thinking and logic of our parents and grandparents generation of schooling. We are a new generation of learners, idealists, and thinkers. Technology and the new information boom has truly made knowledge accessible to all who seek it, but the hard goal is to make education useful, condensed, and exciting for a new generation of learners. Developing smart classrooms that utilize technology and information in a synchronized manner is a great first step in the innovation of our classrooms and giving public education a much needed face lift. Students react very positively to technology and are drawn to its unique capabilities.

This could occur through the use of digital chalk boards, portable text books on smart computers, more interactive projects that utilize the creativity and individuality of young people, more utilization of the internet and computers in and outside of the classroom, among other visionary ideas. Technology has truly opened up an array of doors to reforming our public schools in a way that gets young people back in the groove of learning. Simply ignoring the fact that the majority of students do not enjoy school is not the right way to reform our school system. Instead of continuing in the dark ages of education, we must learn from our young people what they expect and envision in the classroom, what they want to learn and achieve in life.

A lot of people believe that young people are too naïve and inexperienced to know what they want in life, but instead of brushing that aside, we must include students in the discussion of education reform. Although money and finances are a major obstacle for a lot of schools across the nation, accountability and being good stewards of what is available are just as important. I have seen and read about many schools who do just as good, if not better, as those schools with more per pupil spending. Not only do students need to be held accountable, but so do parents, educators, and administrators. We cannot achieve this necessary change in education unless we are willing to sacrifice our time and resources for a greater cause—and that is for the future of our children and our nation. In the words of Nelson Mandela, *"Education is the most powerful weapon which you can use to change the world."*

## Merging Technology in the New Age Is Vital for the Future

As I look around every day at not only myself, but my peers, I notice the great technology era that we are engaging in; texting on our cell phones, checking e-mail wirelessly on the go, posting messages on a friend's walls or tweeting on the go, all the while keeping up with what is happening in the world through online news sites and sometimes the traditional newspaper. We are truly in the information age, where knowledge and ideas are seamlessly converging into one. With all of these new changes, should we be a little nervous and off balance? This is a new and exciting time for all of us that choose to utilize what is out there in terms of technology.

We will continue to see more and more tech items, such as the Apple iPad, which attempt to combine all of those mediums into one: information, entertainment, social networking, and digital content. Our society has become very accustomed to the idea of multi-tasking to the extreme. In a way, we expect that every new product that hits the market should make our lives easier in terms of balancing our schedule and feeding us the information we so desire. A unique new technology developed and released by Microsoft in 2008 called Microsoft Surface, is one example of new technological advances in touch screen, multi-faceted functioning devices.

It is essentially a large LCD computer screen about the size of a small desk which responds to touch (surface computing). It allows users to drag, push, open, spin, stretch, etc. all with the touch of a finger. It allows you to shop online, locate a nearby food joint, and compare items before you purchase them, draw, perform presentations and essentially synchronizes everything you do in a day on one screen. The best way I can describe Microsoft Surface is I-Phone meets Microsoft Live meets Google Map meets CNN's Situation Room. I was thinking to myself, this is it! This is what the future will be like; our technology will essentially mold to our liking, our ideals, our music, our entertainment, our needs and wants.

It will be somewhat frightening at first, but over time we will adjust and be more accustomed to a world of personalized information technology. A device such as Microsoft Surface that will link up with a hand-held device would be the ideal fit for this new tech era. Is this new idea of information and technology scary? Yes. Is it going to make our lives easier and more convenient? That is the hope, but only time will tell. Only our minds, from the fear of failure, will hold us back. The human mind is capable of doing great and astonishing things. We just have to be willing to try, to take risks, to fail and get back up, in order to bring about the idealistic changes that are within our grasps. New technologies from all realms will continue to hit the market, but let us not forget about the simplicities of life—like the beach, napping, taking a walk in a park, among other tranquil and less stressful adventures. Living life to the fullest is not all about what technology we can buy or use, sometimes it is about the small things we seem to forget.

### Green Schools a Role Model for a New Generation

School districts across the nation are slowly implementing cost-efficient and environmentally-sound green schools. Green schools not only help to reduce the use of electricity, water, heating, and cooling, according to an article written by Eva Steele-Saccio, but they also provide students and faculty a new way of learning, as well as a new style. Schools that go "green" use "30 percent less energy and 30 to 50 percent less water than conventional school buildings, and they reduce carbon dioxide emissions by 40 percent," (1). And in total, these healthy and environmentally-sound adjustments are saving schools some $100,000 annually. With those savings more could be used to train teachers, provide new technologies in the classroom, and to create new methods of learning.

There are also many other benefits aside from just the financial savings. The schools themselves have become beacons of what we as Americans should be striving for. These green schools provide an array of "natural light, fresh air, open plans, and multi-use facilities that encourage community involvement" not to mention "test scores rise by 20% and reduce asthma by 39%" (1). These environmentally sound schools provide a learning environment that is innovative, fresh, and creates a sense of hope. However, even with all of these positive success stories about green schools, many school districts believe that they are too costly to build and the projects would take up too much time. But these green schools cost "only 2% more to build" with future savings that outmatch any extra upfront costs.

Many of these green schools are partnering with local resources to become more intertwined with the community and to save money. For instance, one school used the local "YMCA for the school's gym, the public library for books, and local theaters for performance classes" (1). These types of unique and idealistic partnerships bring parents, local businesses, and community leaders back into the mix when it comes to reforming our schools and teaching young people how to be good stewards within their communities. It is truly amazing to see schools being lit with 90% natural sunlight and utilizing recyclable materials to construct classrooms, desks, and so forth.

These new green schools can also involve students in the process by allowing students to research and pick new environmentally sound products and resources as class projects. Our young people need to get back in touch with our environment. For so long now we have forgotten about the beauty and unique qualities of our nation and utilizing the natural resources that are mostly right in our backyards. These new and environmentally sound schools are not only a hope for the future reduction of energy use in our schools and long-term savings overtime, but they are also a hope that one day we can truly inspire and change the very fabric of our culture and society to think GREEN! Source: (1) Magazine: GOOD, Issue 06-Sept/Oct 2007. Author: Eva Steele-Saccio. Title: "Education by Design"

## The New Face of the Internet: Generation Y

Since early 2000, we have seen a great emergence of the Internet rebounding as a new and exciting way of networking once again. Particularly, thanks primarily to sites such as MySpace, which came online in 2003, and Facebook which soon followed in 2006. These sites and many others like them have created a new way of communicating and networking for people of all ages, especially teens and young adults. These social networking sites have allowed people to connect with close friends and relatives like never before, as well as meeting new people with similar beliefs and ideals. And most importantly, they have allowed individuals to share their personal identities with the rest of the world.

Young people relish the value of self worth and individuality, and through this new and exciting transformation of the Internet and networking, they are able to do that. Friends are able to connect with friends on a daily basis, sharing their feelings, beliefs, ideas, favorite movies/music taste, etc., all with the click of the mouse. Young people are no longer being held to the old fashion black journal, but now they have blogs, note posts, and online journals to share their most intimate feelings and moods with those they care about.

Young people have really dived into making the Internet more applicable to their needs and wants. The Internet has become a web of news, sports, entertainment, gossip, connecting with others, and much more for young people today than ever before. Sites like Facebook and Twitter have given users a reason to stay online for hours upon hours a day, doing everything from posting on a friend's wall, to show-casing new pictures from a fun weekend, to updating friends on their daily moods. These social networking sites have essentially opened up the personal lives of millions upon millions of people. It is somewhat amazing to think ten or fifteen years ago, sites such as these would have not been developed due to major privacy concerns. Today we have pushed aside the privacy failures of Internet companies and social networking sites as part of the process of becoming more intertwined with the Internet and information age.

Not only have we come to ultimately accept our flaws, mishaps, and personal issues, in addition we have become even more comfortable with sharing those actions with our friends and total strangers. Every generation has norms of what is acceptable and what is not when it comes to networking and communicating. The current generation, Generation Y, has torn down that barrier and entered unknown territories. Some of the issues that older Internet users face, particularly employers and job recruiters, center on what is culturally acceptable with this generation and how that affects the hiring and retaining of young workers. I have seen and read so many stories of young people getting fired or reprimanded for what they post on their private social networking accounts. Many employers today use blogs and social networking sites as tools to judge potential new employees.

This bears a fundamental question of what is considered too provocative in to-day's ever so engaged, creative, open, and idealistic generation of young people. The Internet has obviously brought billions of people closer together and broken down many barriers in terms of communication, networking, and social activism, but it has also challenged educators, courts, employers, and parents to re-think what Genera-tion Y is all about. I tend to view Generation Y as a generation that is not afraid to speak their mind when asked to, not afraid to take a stand when pushed to, and not afraid to share their hopes and fears. Generation Y embraces the new dimensions of what technology and globalization has brought to it.

The Internet has allowed a generation to slowly but surely find itself, its beliefs, ideals, hopes, dreams, aspirations, and most importantly, its foundation. The founda-tion of Generation Y is one engrained in the words of former President John F.

Kennedy, *"A revolution is coming - a revolution which will be peaceful if we are wise enough; compassionate if we care enough; successful if we are fortunate enough - but a revolution which is coming whether we will it or not. We can affect its character; we cannot alter its inevitability."* This current generation is very much in control of its own destiny. In order to truly grasp it, Generation Y must continue to be the change it wishes to see.

History has shown us that every generation has a medium in which to bring about this change—some generations have used music, television, radio, newspaper, and for this current generation that medium is the Internet. It can be used for either good or evil; my only hope is that all people will use it for good. The day when young people fully use the Internet to rally others to great causes of personal sacrifice is not far away. These great causes will range from reforming health care, education, social security, ending war, destruction, tyranny, poverty and disease, and so much more. Many see this current generation as one which is lost within itself and an ever-growing lack of interest in the problems facing the world. However, I strongly disagree with that assumption, because young people do care. Generation Y cared about 9/11, they care about the Iraq war, they were very much in tune with events such as the Columbine Massacre and the Virginia Tech shooting. And now we have seen young people all across the world lead rallies to bring about democracy throughout the Middle East.

Generation Y has faced very damaging and catastrophic events that have challenged the very fabric of their resolve and ability to stay strong and passionate. In order to figure this all out, one simply has to go on the Internet and look at what this generation has done and still is doing to bring about positive change in the world. Websites such as **www.dosomething.org** and **www.youthnoise.com,** just to name a few, show the passion of young people and their knowledge of the issues that are important today and will be in the future. Most generations, if not all generations before the Internet age, did not have these resources that connect millions of idealistic young people together. This new age of networking and technology is one that is fresh and unknown to all of us. As young people continue to grow older, become more educated, and enter the workforce, I positively believe you will see a new country of leaders and changers.

Educating our young people today on civic involvement and social activism is a vital and important tool in our nation's ability to bring out the best and most adequate use of the Internet. With over 76 million strong, Generation Y is poised to continue to make a splash in politics, business, and the unique world of social networking. Only time will tell how far and historic Generation Y's innovative use of the Internet will take it. In the words of William Pollard, *"Without change there is no innovation, creativity, or incentive for improvement. Those who initiate change will have a better opportunity to manage the change that is inevitable."*

## Stats on Generation Y:

In their book, *Connecting to the Net.Generation: What Higher Education Professionals Need to Know About Today's Students,* Reynol Junco and Jeanna Mastrodicasa (2007) found that in a survey of 7,705 college students in the US:

- 97% own a computer
- 94% own a cell phone
- 76% use Instant Messaging
- 15% of IM users are logged on 24 hours a day/7 days a week
- 34% use websites as their primary source of news
- 28% own a blog and 44% read blogs
- 49% download music using peer-to-peer file sharing
- 75% of students have a Facebook account
- 60% own some type of expensive portable music and/or video device such as an iPod

## The Re-Education of Education Reform

Lack of creativity, idealism, structured classes, motivated students, parents, and teachers, and stuck in 20th century thinking describes the current U.S. educational structure. How do we reform our education system and win back the hearts and minds of a lost generation? Having worked in the Washington, DC public school system for almost two years, I have seen up close and personal the failures of our current education system. A system that was created for 20th Century thinking has fallen miserably behind the rest of the world. We all know there are hundreds, if not thousands, of crumbling schools with a lack of infrastructure, teaching materials, qualified teachers, and a myriad of other adversities. However, those are not the only issues with our current education system.

The thinking in which our school systems across the nation operate is sorely misplaced and perpetuating the problem of creating a future of young people who will be ill prepared for the challenges of the future. Firstly, we have created a student vs. student education system in which every student is for him or herself. The best letter grade wins—no matter how the student got to that point. If you cannot keep up, then too bad, it is a dog eat dog world. Sure, this way of thinking works in our military vs. an enemy or a political campaign, but it should not be the type of thinking we instill in our children.

Our school system should be functioning in a manner in which every student is given an equal opportunity to learn in first-rate classrooms with caring adults who try to pull the best ideals out of every student, not just a select few. Students should be challenged to work together in teams, solving problems, creating solutions, and thinking outside of the box. They should be experimenting, getting hands-on learning from professionals across many career fields from science to theater to government.

Our young people deserve an education system that is working for them, not against them. A system that is fighting to raise standards, while simultaneously challenging parents to be actively involved and engaged in their child's education. Our country's future depends on the success or failure of our education system. Secondly, we cannot expect our children to learn when many schools resemble a prison. When a school is mostly white walls, with very little artwork or positive words, without technological advances, or a clean and well-stocked library—we cannot expect our children to want to learn. School should be a breeding ground for a young person's ideals, beliefs, culture, and should motivate them to excel at their highest aspirations. Learning should not be thought of as a place only for "nerds"; learning is the foundation of civilization as we know it. When students are in a building that resembles the hope and prosperity we want to instill in them, we can then challenge them to be successful, to work hard, never give up, and live life to the fullest.

This brings me to a third vital point to re-invigorate our education system—creating a challenging curriculum that is based on a strong core philosophical belief that in order to learn, students must be given the best educational materials, well-trained and excited teachers, and lessons that tie real-world experiences and learning into a student's everyday life. Regardless of what we think, students need to know that what they are learning will benefit them some way down the road. Students must feel as though they are being challenged, not just because it's their teachers' job, but because it will better their future. We must be able to tie all of these things together to create a new paradigm in which our children are taught and how to engage them in the learning process. Setting tough standards and living up to those standards is vital to the success of a new 21st century education system.

We cannot fail our young people, the stakes are too high and time is running out. We need to promote cooperation, teamwork, creativity, culture, idealism, and remind all Americans that for our nation to stay relevant in the 21st century we must reform our educational system and way of thinking! We have to win back the hearts and minds of our students—it can be done and most importantly it must be done.

## The Big Picture of Education

Every morning before I headed to my City Year School, I picked up the free daily newspaper in Washington, DC called the *Express*. One day as I flipped through the paper, there was an article in the back that immediately caught my attention and inspired me. The article was titled "Big Picture schools let students direct their own curricula." Part of the mission of Big Picture Schools is "to lead vital changes in education, both in the United States and internationally, by generating and sustaining innovative, personalized schools that work in tandem with the real world of the greater community." Big Picture Schools is a truly innovative and amazing new educational institution created to motivate and teach at-risk young people. There are "no teachers, no homework, no tests, and no grades." Students are in control of their curricula and their future plans for life after high school, and there is no cost to attend one of these schools, as they are funded by the school district in which the Big School resides.

Instead of being called a teacher, the class instructor is called an adviser, who works with the same class for all four years of high school and coordinates all of the lessons. During the school week, students spend two-days of that time working at real-life internships that fit their career goals and ideals. Each student must apply to at least one college after graduating and be accepted. Big Picture schools "emphasize work in the real world, portfolios, oral presentations and intense relationships between students and advisers." Students are seen first and foremost as creative individuals, who excel when challenged and given a chance to pursue their own dreams and goals. Big Picture schools are "now about 7,500 students in 16 states" and have "a 92 percent graduation rate--sending nearly 95 percent of their students for post-secondary learning."

This innovative and unique approach is a complete 360 away from traditional education, which is focused on standardized testing and placing every student into different learning categories—such as proficient, basic, or above proficiency. The traditional education method does not treat students as idealistic individuals to give them a chance to dream big and truly reach for their goals and aspirations. During my time as a City Year corps member, I saw every day the plight of students who felt as though they were being left out in the cold and not truly being given a chance to learn. Students deserve the best education possible and to be treated as individuals, not as delinquents. Young people deserve innovative learning that mixes technology, in-class instruction, caring adults, real world experiences, and independent learning as a means to improve their futures.

According to the Silent Epidemic Summit that was held in Washington, DC in 2007, "80 percent of students who dropped out of school said they would have likely graduated if their schools had provided them with real-world learning opportunities." Our country needs more innovative school models like Big Picture Schools to infuse a new energy and spark in the minds of our young people. Every child deserves a chance to learn and succeed, no matter how poor or rich he or she may be. I truly hope for the day when education is about creativity and will continue to work towards an education system that opens new doors and opportunities for a new generation.

*Information for this essay was gathered from Express, a publication of the Washington Post-Thursday, December 18th, 2008.*

## Living in a Facebook World

The magical confluence of information, communication, and personalization is Facebook and social networking in general. Creations such as Facebook have opened up a new paradigm for our generation and have completely altered the idea of what is expected from us as individuals. Firstly, the mass amount of information that social networking has brought upon us is quite amazing. Users are able to not only place their whole life for others to see, but also are allowed to view others lives—friends and strangers alike.

There was a time when talking to strangers was not the best idea, however, in today's world, as long as it stays within the realm of social networking, it is seen as an advantage—you meet new people, make new connections, and find out more information than you really ever needed to know. Our society today is driven by information—what people know, what they want to know, and how it benefits them.

We live in a 24 hour news cycle society, touch screen communication devices, constant e-mailing, texting, blogging, wireless/web communications, and a diverse link to our international counterparts that was unforeseen even 10 years ago. I will not even attempt to argue if this is good or bad—I think with anything, especially technology, it lies in the eye of the beholder.

Secondly, social networking has brought about a new means of communication to go along with our smart phones, e-mail, and instant messaging platforms. The fact that users can communicate with someone in Germany just as fast as they can with a classmate across the room, is quite astonishing. Communication today is the direct result of a powerful need—mostly due to globalization—for consistent creative discussions back and forth between companies, entrepreneurs, government, and the like. We, as a people, are lucky enough to see innovation at its best, made for civilian use so we too can partake in this unique 21$^{st}$ century technological journey. Many of us fret when we misplace our cell phone or lose our Internet connection due to a storm—as if it is the end of the world. We have been so spoiled by the new technologies of our generation; many of us clearly could not live without it. And finally, social networking has brought about personalization of our own identities, likes and dislikes, personal philosophies, and has allowed us to share them with the rest of the world quite freely. If you have the right tools and knowledge, you could quite possibly find out everything you ever wanted to know about an individual just by looking at their Facebook or Twitter profile, or any of the other myriad of social networking sites.

This personalization has cut down the first question most of us ask when we meet someone for the first time either subconsciously or out loud: who are you? We can figure that out before the first hand shake and dive right into the important details. It is especially quite useful for employers in the 21$^{st}$ Century as they determine if a potential employee is a right fit for their company and its long-term vision. And most importantly, you can do the same—in a way it cuts out the middle man and connects both user and employer simultaneously. In conclusion, living in a Facebook world clearly has its benefits—the ability to link up with friends old and new, to communicate with a far away world, to show society who you are as a unique individual and the hopes, dreams, and fears you may hold about the future, and the ability to bring social change from a desk. If used for good, this new-found congruence of networking and technology can usher in a new era of innovators, social entrepreneurs, thinkers, and inventors all from a personal workspace. I would challenge you to take advantage of this unique time in our history and use it to make a positive difference in the lives of others. Find out what makes you churn creatively, your own talents and gifts, and meet others who share those same faiths, ideas, and indebted values to change the world so a future generation can live in a cleaner, safer, and even more innovative society than we do today.

## Equal Education Still a Dream for Many

Imagine a place where ideas are created, dreams are lived, and hands-on interactive experiences are the cornerstone of learning. An education foundation in which children are seen, not merely as test-taking robots, but as active participants and equals in their own educational journey now and in the future. A place filled with excitement, interactive learning, cooperation, and respect—where theaters and auditoriums are places of improvisation, acting, and being—science labs to experiment and create, art centers to draw and imagine. For many schools this is not just an imagination, but a reality. Children are truly able to see themselves in the work they accomplish. They are able to learn not merely by just seeing, but also by doing—they are not told to just dream big, but they can live their dreams now in the present. Every young mind is such a precious, delicate, and important idea that must be nurtured and expanded. The young mind must be challenged and tested, excited and calmed.

While in City Year I had the opportunity to work with young people who did not have all of these necessary resources, let alone the motivation to push themselves academically. However, they came to school ready for whatever the day brought them, either good or bad. They learned and made-do with what they had and when they succeeded, the smile on their faces made my work and the work of my peers even more gratifying and heartwarming. Even though they did not always listen to me the first time or even the third time, they knew that I was there to make their lives just a little bit better, to help them go farther than they thought was possible and little did they know, they challenged me to do the same—to stand up in the face of adversity, to live everyday as though it was my last, and to never allow the little things to tear away my sense of being and belief in social change. All of my students had a purpose in life and if they were given the same resources as many of their fellow peers across this nation, they too would be able to attend the best colleges and attain the best jobs in the future. However, as of now, they are at a deep disadvantage in the quest for equal educational and life opportunities.

Standardized testing would not be a necessity if school districts and our nation would invest in the resources, teachers, infrastructure, and commitment to learning that we all know is possible and necessary for the future success of our country in this globalized economy. When rural and inner city youth have been trained to expect mediocrity or at worse failure, why should they show respect, concern, love, or a true passion for learning when they know there is no light at the end of the tunnel? Instead they are forced to see education as just another long step to failure, just as many of their parents and relatives have experienced. It is so hard to see hope, prosperity, or a chance for success when no one believes in you.

My students have truly been inspired by the Obama presidency and it gives them hope that they too can become something great in our society, no matter the color of their skin or their current socio-economic status. However, this moment will not last forever, which is why we must continue to show all children the path to success is achieved through positive actions and self-development. When it comes to inspiring, challenging, and growing the minds of our future doctors, entrepreneurs, scientists, thinkers, artists, and so forth—from Pre-K through college, they must be immersed in a full spectrum of educational opportunities and cultural awareness. This is where our present and future must lead us. Our commitment to learning must be unwavering, wide-ranging, diverse, challenging, motivating, and without excuses or acceptance of failure. We should expect nothing less than perfection from our students, parents, teachers, staff, and school administrators—both locally, state-wide, and nationally. Every child has a purpose—no matter where they live, the color of their skin, or their social and economic background. They are the future, so are we planning to accept failure or mark a turning point in providing every child with a true and excellent education? We must act for the sake of our nation and for the sake of every child who dares to dream.

## Interactive Social Media and Its Effect on Society

In our generation there has been an influx of social networking and social media outlets ranging from AOL, Yahoo, Friendster, YouTube, MySpace, Facebook, and now Twitter. Many still wonder what exactly does the creation of these social media devices mean for ordinary people.

Firstly, they allow citizens to express themselves to the rest of the world. In the past the only way to express yourself was to a.) Write a letter that may or may not reach its destination, b.) Write for a newspaper, magazine, or even publish your own book with your thoughts on important topics, or c.) Aim for fame in hopes of money, power, and influence. However, in today's fast paced, news saturated social bubble, people are able to express themselves freely, openly, and interactively in many different social arenas online. You no longer need millions of dollars to make an impact or have connections to a high-powered executive to be a part of this new era of social interactive media (although those things help).

Secondly, this new era of social media merges like-minded people and industries together in an effort to make products, services, and even the news more consumer driven. Companies such as Microsoft and CNN, just to name a few, are able to connect with users from all over the U.S. and the world to test new product ideas, news stories, and get instant feedback. A former CNN personality, Rick Sanchez, hosted a daily news show and took many of his questions and story ideas from social networking users, ranging from Facebook to Twitter. And even Facebook, which has revolution-ized the way users communicate with one another and our media-driven culture, learned first-hand about instant feedback, when their own users responded quickly with criticism to a myriad of site changes and privacy concerns.

Lastly, interactive social media has given a new and empowered voice to entrepre-neurs, writers, thinkers, and ordinary people to create their own hopes and dreams right before the eyes of millions. Information moves much smoother; ideas and criticism come quickly, and all users are connected to one another in a split second allowing for constant updates and communication. As the future progresses I imagine more interactive social media frameworks coming along and becoming more prevalent in hand-held devices, vehicles, homes, and work. This will allow for an almost 24/7 communication link between people, business, news, and technology. What the future holds—only time will tell, and it may be coming faster than we think.

## Social Media and the Future of News

Media today is becoming more interactive and engaging than ever before. Many would say it is about time, while others would say media organizations have been too late to recognize this changing landscape. Over the last two years alone over 120 traditional print newspapers have closed down, causing the loss of thousands of jobs and many are left scratching their heads on what to do next. And it is not just local and state newspapers, even national newspapers like the Washington Post and the New York

Times have had to cut personnel and salaries to keep up with the millions of dollars in advertising losses due to lack of readership. While some, like the Wall Street Journal, realized just in time that print media was diverging ever so quickly with the Internet, most have not. There is still something magical about turning through the crisp pages of a newspaper and mundane when scrolling with a mouse online to check out the day's latest news. Although I do not believe print will entirely evaporate, I believe there will be substantial changes over the next decade in terms of social media and how people engage and interact with print and online journalism and social media.

I still remember being in middle school and starting the student newspaper and in high school where I had the opportunity to write my own weekly column. Little did I know blogging and social networking sites such as Twitter, Blogger, and Facebook would be leading the way in how we attain information and interact with those entities in which the information is being delivered. Even while in high school, I was a part of the social media bubble, participating in chat rooms, message boards, and interactive news and opinion sites such as Youth Noise, but even then it was not something most people were engaged in during the early 2000s. How media companies adjust with this changing landscape and their ability to connect with readers and viewers will be instrumental in driving the future direction of social media and community engagement. Some media companies that are still highly involved with print media will begin charging for their online content, much like the Wall Street Journal does today, while others will cut down circulation or even end their print capacities completely and take to the web.

There is also the advent of citizen journalism, where ordinary people are just as capable of reporting the news from their own perspectives via blog sites or social networking sites without a corporate filter to control their message. Many major media companies, such as CNN with their iReport feature, have embraced the idea of utilizing amateur journalists to add a more community and inclusive fill to their reporting apparatus. With the increased use of camera phones, tablet PC's like the iPad, and video sites such as YouTube, it is quite understandable why ordinary citizens have been very important in the advent of social media and the changing media landscape. The Internet has been great in bringing together ideas, news, and information like never before. The sources are infinite and the ability to engage with one another is even more accepted and expected in today's society.

However, it is still vital that as a citizenry we never forget the importance of un-biased and in depth reporting to keep our government honest and to provide the information we need as a society to have a clear and neutral reporting of the facts. I look forward to seeing how mass media companies fuse with the ever growing interactive media generation and how we as a people become even more in depth and engaged with community reporting and information gathering. Technology and the Internet will both have a profound effect on the future of media and how people attain, share, and decipher information.

## How Education Today is Killing Our Kids
## and What We Can Do to Change It

Ok, yes the title is a little drastic, but it is catchy! All joking aside, education today is creating a seismic schism between the creative development and engagement of our young students and the reality of standardized, statistical orientated teaching and learning. When you look back at your days in class, how many times did you feel as though what you were learning had nothing to do with your eventual dreams or goals for your life? Or the feeling that schools were so focused on getting the best standardized test scores that the idea of allowing students to be creative was thrown completely under the bus? Sadly, it is worse today than ever before. Pablo Picasso once said, *"All children are artists. The problem is how to remain an artist once he grows up."* I believe this resonates loudly today with the ever-growing iron fist of standardized testing. Students are no longer seen as creative human beings that are capable of so much when given the opportunity and the resources to mold and build their own futures.

Sir Ken Robinson, Ph.D., one of the most well-known experts on creativity, innovation and human resources, puts it like this: *"In a nutshell, it's that we're born with immense natural talents, but our institutions, especially education, tend to stifle many of them and as a result we are fomenting a human and economic disaster."* He goes on to argue that with the advent of mass testing of students, arts and creative development have all been downgraded and teachers are forced to adhere to rigid testing standards and regulations. In a recent 2009 report by the National Commission on Teaching and America's Future, "one of every three new teachers will leave the profession within five years" and "more than a third of the nation's 3.2 million teachers could retire over the next four years."

In order to keep this national tragedy from causing major economic and educational disruptions in our nation's schools, teachers must be given the tools, resources, and leeway to work with students on an individual level, instead of the traditional means of learning, i.e. chalk/white boards and lectures. In our ever growing tech-savvy society, social networking and innovation are changing the way we get information and how we share that information with others. We must do more to engage and empower our young people to come out of their shells and explore their own creative and innovative talents with teachers leading the way.

In a recent study by Gallup to measure the hope, engagement, and well-being of America's students, in which 70,078 students in grades 5 through 12 from 335 schools and 59 districts located in 18 states and the District of Columbia were polled, the results were quite powerful.

Half of students are hopeful; these students possess numerous ideas and abundant energy for the future. The other 50% are stuck or discouraged, lacking the ideas and energy they need to navigate problems and reach goals.

Half of students are engaged; they are highly involved with and enthusiastic about school. The other half of students are either going through the motions of school or actively undermining the teaching and learning process.

Nearly two-thirds of students are thriving; they think about their present and future life in positive terms, and they tend to be in good health and have strong social support. Just over one-third of students are struggling or suffering.

25% of responding students meet the criteria for classification of hopeful, engaged, and thriving. These students have abundant energy and ideas about the future and are enthusiastic about school and what it has to offer.

Generally, this report tells us that we have much more work to do to give our young people the resources and opportunities to share with us their creative talents and to live a life that they enjoy, that is not based on parental or cultural expectations of what they should or should not do with their lives in the realm of career and education. The expectation for most students is that they should finish high school, finish college, get a job, raise a family, and retire. However, this expectation is rooted in the decades past, which no longer applies. Educational objectives and wanted outcomes must measure up to the needs and wants of today's generation without barring students from engaging in the arts and real experiential learning outside of the classroom.

We must not kid ourselves and must finally recognize that we are in a national crisis. In a recent hearing held by the US House of Representatives Committee on Education and Labor, experts testified that "only about 70 percent of students graduate from high school with a regular high school diploma" and "in the 50 largest cities, only 53% of students graduate on time." When students are not in the classroom learning and truly being able to reach their goals and dreams, it affects all of us. The McKinsey Corporation recently found "that if minority student performance had reached white students by 1998, GDP in 2009 would have been between $310 billion and $525 billion higher or approx. 2 to 4 percent of GDP." We cannot continue to ignore the economic and cultural impacts of a failed education system that is truly leaving out and ignoring many of our most desperate youth.

Education today is primarily focused on right and wrong—or simply put: failure. There is no longer a view in most public schools that making mistakes is a means to learn from them and to grow as an individual and as a creative talent. Students are given rigid standards by way of standardized tests, and if they do not meet those prescribe standards they are considered a failure. We stigmatize those students--they are called dumb, ADD, ADHD, special, etc. Instead we should try and figure out what those students' creative talents are—what they want to learn, who they are as people, their hopes and dreams. And with that information, design a curriculum that is based on a student's goals and ideals, without getting rid of a strong curriculum that includes math, science, reading, writing, etc. I believe that every child deserves a well-rounded education so they have the opportunity to decide their own future aspirations, and not the system deciding for them.

What if we measured student success based on the outcome of the individual student's goals and creative talents and not based on a one-size-fits-all test? What if we taught students self-leadership, personal development, and creative exploration along with a core college prep curriculum? Let us not merely measure student success on what past generations believed was important, but let us instead explore the realm of what has not yet been discovered. There is so much to learn from our young people and I believe that the future of education and America's social and economic status in the world depends on.

One of my favorite collections of words by Sir Ken Robinson is this: *"Education is about developing human beings, and human development is not mechanical or linear. It is organic and dynamic."* He is saying education cannot be forced, it cannot be spoon-fed, but must come up from the hearts, souls, and minds of our young people and their own quest for purpose and creative freedom.

## The Other Deficit in America: Middle Class Opportunity

There is no misunderstanding that America faces a major debt crisis that could dictate the future success of our nation's economy for years to come. We must do more to reform and restructure our entitlement programs, such as Social Security, Medicare, and Medicaid. We also must do more to cut spending—both discretionary and non-discretionary and reform government financed housing agencies Freddie and Fannie. Our nation faces very important and monumental questions about the direction of social progress and who we will become in the next twenty years as a society. Future decisions on expenditures will dictate not only our national priorities, but our treatment of middle and low income Americans of all races and backgrounds.

The current recession has placed a lethal burden on families across America. States have cut education spending and reduced social safety nets for millions of individuals and families. New taxes have been created and old ones increased to close budget deficits all across the country. Many American families, if not most, have been experiencing budget cuts and deficit reductions for years now. Families all across this country have had to cut their own spending, deal with bankruptcies and foreclosures, lost investments, and dwindling college funds for their children. The wealth gap in this country has been expanding for decades, as has educational inequality. The last ten years was filled with stagnant income growth and a structural system that encouraged unusually high risk taking and relaxed regulations within the financial industry and many others, i.e. oil companies. What we have seen is a return to the need for responsible living, spending, and saving all across America. We must also return to protecting and promoting the rebirth of American innovation in education, energy, technology, science, and manufacturing.

The other deficit in this country is our lack of priorities aimed at the middle class. Our leaders for too long have been more concerned with propping up the elite, corporations, and those with wealth, instead of building a stronger system of economic independence and sustainability from the bottom up. When we empower and educate people of all races and economic ladders to take control of their own futures, we are building a better society and economy that works for all people instead of just the few and privileged. To simply utilize draconian spending cuts and tax increases that will primarily hurt those who have already endured these actions for far too long neglects the fact we must do more in this country to increase opportunity and prosperity for millions of Americans left in the darkness.

Our priorities must once again realize that we are all intricately linked as a nation—the success of this country at the end of the day, as evident by the recent near collapse of our financial system, is not merely big banks and corporations, but it is the people that depend on these very same institutions for their livelihoods. The success of the American people should not depend on the fall or rise of corporate America. Revitalizing our urban and rural communities, re-developing closed manufacturing plants, investing in new sectors, increasing small business loans and entrepreneur courses, improving our education system, continuously reducing the cost of health care & restructuring the tax system, and promoting economic and social sustainability are all vital in building a balanced and sustainable economy.

When all Americans have opportunities to create and grow their own small businesses, to own an affordable home, save college funds for their children, to invest and save for retirement, and go about their lives knowing that their government and the policies that were created benefit their livelihoods, that is when we will have created a sustainable and flourishing economy. There is no doubt we have a financial deficit of monumental proportions, but let us not forget the faces and the families behind those numbers. Let us not forget our own humanity and the ideals by which this nation was founded and the promise that all Americans are created equal and given the opportunity to pursue happiness no matter where they reside in this nation, not just for those on Wall Street, but most importantly, those on Main Street.

## Sustainability, Sustainability, Sustainability!

Republicans are talking about freedom, Democrats are talking about justice, and Libertarians are talking about liberty. These are all wonderful and vitally important foundations of American society in both legal and practical terms. However, each person has his or her own belief on exactly what those three American ideals actually entail. Freedom for one man may be bondage for another, justice for one may not mean justice for all, and liberty may apply to certain freedoms and institutions and not others. And most importantly, none of these majestic ideals provide for a sustainable, healthy, and plentiful earth. In order to ensure the people of America and the planet can survive for generations, we must rally around the core principle of sustainability. We all know that fossil fuels are finite and toxic for our environment;

we know that too much debt is bad for our economic prosperity; we know that clean energy is both doable and necessary; we know that our nation's infrastructure needs rebuilding—from roads to hospitals to schools; and we know that a society that values human longevity and positive interactions between man and our ecosystem is vital for the future survival of the human race.

However, we as a people have been unable to make the hard choices to preserve our society as it is today for future generations, even with all of its imperfections. We have dealt with environmental disasters—both manmade and natural, we have survived plagues and outbreaks, we have defeated dictators and despots, and we have brought a divided nation together as a united union. Our biggest challenge of all is squarely staring us in the face and quite honestly, kicking our butt. Our leaders have been unable to legislate effectively with long-term thinking and planning in mind, the American people have been plagued with the same short-sightedness and inability to make the sacrifices necessary on behalf of future generations, and international institutions have been unable to corral nations together around a common theme of global sustainability. If there is one issue we should at least agree on, it is that in order for society to survive, real and sustainable social change must occur. We must use innovative ideas, science, and technology to create the solutions necessary for long-term growth and prosperity. If we continue to allow corporate interest to overtake the interest of the people and the well-being of our society, we will have failed future generations in our quest to create a sustainable environment.

It is not too late, but the time for action is approaching rapidly and in unpredictable order. If we continue on our path of destruction, relegating current manageable societal issues to future generations, and failing to comprehend the gravity of our excess abuses, the hand of man, with all of its progress and intelligence, will seal its own doom and fate. Simply talking about the issues we face is no longer enough, we must take stark action and be prepared to deal with the short and medium term consequences for long-term gain. We must continue to educate ourselves, learn about the issues affecting our society, engage those around us, and act. My hope is that the American people and our leaders will put aside the petty politics and rhetoric and actually seek to promote and create the policies necessary for long-term sustainable social change. America must lead in this endeavor and if we do, others will follow.

## Making the Challenges of Education Reform Real for Students

When we talk about education reform and achievement there is always a gaping hole in making it relevant for young people and their parents. We have a lot of intelligent and truly caring people in conference rooms sifting through data, debating, writing press releases, and deciding what they think is best in terms of education policy—but most of the time it is never made real for the students or their parents. It simply becomes another statistic that guides a new initiative that promises to make a dramatic impact in the lives of our young people. At what point do we realize that we have failed to truly change the direction of our educational system, that we must do more to engage our young people inside and outside of the classroom? There is a valuable dynamic in having a conversation with young people about their futures, their success, and their livelihoods. A typical young person does not follow the news or read the newspaper; they are typically not engaged in the daily, weekly, and monthly education policy battles, but they should be.

It is vital that we tell students that they will make less money without a high school diploma or a college degree and that the achievement gap between white and minority students is growing, that almost half of black students will drop out of high school. We must give them the knowledge so they too can be a part of shaping their destiny, so that they are not just another statistic or line on a graph. Adults find it easy sometimes to see a bump on a graph or a couple percentage point bump in reading scores—but the real question is do our students feel it, do they see it, and are they responding to the challenge? Having a dialogue with our young people about the challenges within their communities, their schools, and the sort of future we want them to have is paramount. And that discussion should never end—it must be ongoing and evolving—and most importantly, as a nation we must provide the resources and support to ensure they can meet those challenges. Expectations can only be reached and exceeded once we take a holistic approach to bring young people and parents into the fold.

Mentoring programs, community service, social and cultural projects, and an increased emphasis on hands-on learning are all key to reaching our young people—and to drive them to take full control of their present and future lives. This is not a short-term project, it is one which requires a sustained effort by all stakeholders—parents, teachers, school administrators, counselors, community and church leaders, and business and government leaders. Educating our young people must be the top priority of all stakeholders for the foreseeable future to ensure America does not lose its competitive edge in innovation and economic development. When young people gain a deeper understanding of themselves, the challenges they face; their goals and the necessary steps they must take to achieve them, we as a nation will be moving in the right direction. Education reform must not begin and end in a conference room and a graph, it must extend to the hearts and minds of every single young person who dares to live a life worth dreaming.

## Education in America and the Challenges We Face

When most people think about education reform they tend to gravitate towards standardized testing, teacher performance, college readiness, school building renovations, and student achievement inside the classroom. These are all vital pieces to the puzzle and the challenges to creating a higher standard of achievement within our nation's schools. However, even with all of these challenges and even with modest successes that many school districts have achieved with a laser-like focus—we fail to address the social and developmental needs of our most challenged communities and youth. Drugs, violence, untreated mental and physical disabilities, and poor parenting have all played a role in the deteriorating situation in the black community.

In America alone three out of every 10 students drop out of high school and for African-Americans it is almost fifty percent. The achievement gap continues to widen between white students and minorities. Even with this dark cloud hovering over millions of young people, there have been some local bright spots as of late. In a Chicago public school, Englewood Urban Prep Academy, where all of the students are male and African-American, every single one of them graduated and got accepted into a college. These are the type of success stories many communities want to read about and use as a means to transfer those successes to other schools.

Since President Obama took office, his administration has instituted a renewed focus on innovative change within the education system with the Race to the Top program. This program is providing $4.35 billion in competitive grants for states to compete for. In order to be eligible for the awards, states and school districts must show how they are measuring teacher performance and student achievement, turning around low-performing schools, and most importantly, utilizing innovative tools and resources to improve educational outcomes. The effects of a poorly educated generation may not be felt as immediate as a recession or housing bubble, but the long-term effects are just as damaging, if not more, for America's long-term eco-nomic and social standing in the world.

We must do more to not only better educate our young people through improved curricula, teacher accountability standards, and student performance tools, but we must do more to develop and motivate our young people. Young people today more than ever before are more engaged and in tune with the world around them. Howev-er, if we do not attempt to develop and hone that engagement we will fail at truly providing a holistic and well-rounded educational experience. Challenging our young people to give back through community service, to complete challenging hands-on projects that push them to question who they are and what they stand for, to help develop their short and long term goals in life, to motivate and help develop their leadership abilities, and to look at local, national, and global issues of social, cultural, and economic importance to form their own thoughts and observations, are all of utmost importance in the development of our young people.

Once a young person believes in him or herself, and has not just the educational components, but the life skills necessary to not just finish high school, but to excel and to live out his or her dreams, we as a nation will have achieved our objective of educating and empowering every child. And we must not start off with the premise of impossibility, but must instead look deep within our own souls and question exactly what we stand for and what sort of America and globe we wish to build in the coming years and decades. Will we build a society that values some over others? That pits one group of people against another and that sees educational and life development as a privilege and not a right? Our nation cannot stand on hollow ground, nor can we stand with a society that is half-educated.

Providing equal opportunity is not just about one half getting more than the other, it is about providing opportunities to excel in every aspect of life, school, and career to every child. Economic prosperity is not just good for one, it is good for all—it is good for our nation and for the world as a whole. As someone who has worked with inner city youth who come from varied backgrounds, there is always hope in a child—no matter where they come from or their socio-economic back-ground, but that is not to say those challenges do not create another barrier to educational and life excellence. If you provide a child with a glimmer of hope, with a promise that everything will be done that is humanely possible to help them succeed, and actually provide the resources, support, and tools they need—they will meet and exceed those expectations every step of the way.

Parents must challenge their children to believe in themselves and to see the direct link between educational success and life success—that through their hard work and perseverance there will be light at the end of the tunnel, and their life goals will come true. No one has succeeded in life by quitting at the starting line—the road is tough, bumpy, and unpredictable—there will not always be a shiny light of happiness at every turn, but the promise of tomorrow is greatly improved with a determined sense of purpose and humanity. We must all take a stake in this great challenge— donating our time, resources, and skills to make a positive difference. All of our hands must get dirty in order to provide the children of our nation an endearing, hopeful, and successful chance to live a fruitful life now and forever.

# 2
# HAVE FAITH IN YOURSELF

*"Faith... is the art of holding on to things your reason*
*once accepted, despite your changing moods."*
--C.S. Lewis

Lacking the encouragement, motivation, and belief in one's self is the first characteristic of failure and lack of success. However, failure is not a means to quit altogether,
it simply means you have learned what not to do and how far you still have left to
grow and achieve. It is hard to convince others of one's talents, beliefs, and ideals if
they first do not have faith in themselves. This chapter will seek to identify the
meaning of faith in today's society and how faith is vital to the success or failure of
one's life and ultimate purpose.

A) The Power of Faith.
B) The Importance of Positive Thinking.
C) Failure is never the end.
D) Believing in your ultimate purpose.

## Living the Dream of a Life Just Beginning

Have you ever wondered what your life would be like if you had chosen a different
path? Maybe instead of going to college you moved to Los Angeles to become an
actor, or you followed a different dream rather than the one you are living now. What
if you had the chance to live a different dream, a different chance to be the person
you wanted to be? Now, to be clear, that does not mean that you are not happy
where you are now or even that your other goal in life would have ended up any
differently, but simply put, to try something in life you had the same amount of love

and energy for. We now live in a society that says if you are good with something, stick with it! But what if you are good at multiple things? How are you supposed to pick? Which good is the best choice? Is the goal in life you should follow the one that will make you the most money or give you the most happiness, or is it the one that your family believes is the right one for you? If you have multiple talents in life, do not be afraid to try all of them!

I am constantly thinking about the meaning and purpose of living our deepest and most intimate aspirations. There has to be so much more than just going to college, getting a job, having a family, and dying! Life is about being extremely happy, having great family and friends, trying new things, having a strong religious faith, and not giving up! Every day is a new beginning, a new life of sorts that is fresh and as new as blooming flowers in the spring.

People always ask me, why do you have so much energy and motivation to do everything you do? Well, simply put, because I know I am on this Earth for a purpose and I want to live everyday to press forward to be that human being I was created to be, wherever that may take me! Life is constantly a mystery, with many of us searching and exploring each and every single day for the answers. Yes, we will all make mistakes, we will all have regrets, and we will all have times of joy and success. That is what life is all about. One thing life is not about is giving up and succumbing to being less than what we are capable of achieving. Do not let age, disability, race, or any other perceived handicap be a block in your path to dreaming and living.

If you want to become a doctor, dream it and be it; if you want to sky dive, take a deep breath and go for it; and if you want to change the world, find a niche/problem and fight for a solution! Live everyday to the fullest and do not let the worries of the world get you down, because in the end, the only thing that matters is where your heart and soul are. Just breathe, imagine, reflect, and do it all over again, you never know what you may find!

### Success and Failure Go Together

As you are studying for your upcoming exam or writing a new business plan for a café you are planning to open, all that goes through your head is success! You are thinking about all the great possibilities that could come out of the end result. With this higher grade I'll get a bigger allowance, or once I get this new café open I'll finally get that new Mercedes-Benz I always wanted. But in reality, what if success does not come? What if the dreams and goals you had come crashing down on you without notice, due to some unexpected circumstance? Would you be prepared for failure in any part of your life, whether it is family stability, financial, or emotional? Life is not just about success, it is also about failure. Very few people have succeeded in life without experiencing some sort of failure. We are able to learn right from wrong and good from bad—all from the experiences we have in our lives, or even the experiences we see other people close to us going through within their own lives.

Without mapping out all of the possibilities, good or bad, in your daily ventures and goals, you are leaving yourself vulnerable and short changed to fully reach your ultimate goal, whether it is an A+ on a test or starting your own business. Pretty much every business has a worst case scenario for all of the potential what ifs, as does the government, such as NASA, and any other agency or business that plans to succeed in whatever their objective may be. So why aren't we as individuals planning for the potential of failure in our lives? Creating a success and failure plan is as easy as writing down your daily thoughts or answering the phone. Seeing and understanding the possible failures in your life and goals is one way to better understand who you are, what you can achieve, what you need help in, and how you can help others. It is ensuring that you have both feet forward and that you are ready for any and all challenges that may interfere with your ultimate goals of success.

Success is not merely something that happens overnight or without glitches. Many of us fall down multiple times before we are able to fully pick ourselves up and understand how we can solve the problem. Therefore, by being proactive rather than reactive, we are able to save time, money, effort, and energy. No one is perfect on this Earth and we should never try to be. We should be living our wildest dreams out in reality and trying our hardest to be the best we can be. With that expectation is the responsibility to see both sides of the ball—failure and success. Just because you may fail in an attempt to achieve a goal does not mean it was not meant to be or you should just give up and throw in the towel.

It simply means that you need to fix something; you need to re-evaluate what is wrong and right in your life, as well as those around you. You need to better understand who you are as a person and what you really want to achieve. Do not fear who you are and what you hold as your life long mission(s) in life, because in the end we are all striving for the same over-arching goal: Success! In the words of the great Martin Luther King Jr.: *"Even if I knew that tomorrow the world would go to pieces, I would still plant my apple tree."*

### Overcoming the Greatest Challenge of All: You

When I walk around Barnes and Noble, I can only imagine the work and time so many authors have put in when writing their masterpieces. It is truly amazing to imagine the creativity and idealism that authors must have in order to sustain such writings and to truly empower others to do the same. There is so much power in reading the thoughts and ideals of others who have treaded similar or different paths. You can learn about the history of Mesopotamia or the trials and tribulations of great leaders such as Nelson Mandela or partake in the delicious recipes of the White House Chef, all in a day. Knowledge is such a powerful tool and it causes us to step out of our comfort zones and what we think we know in order to truly understand the realities and truths of life. The world is a mysterious place with interesting and provocative challenges in which we must continuously question everything before our eyes. We must be willing to open our minds to new experiences and ideals, while not necessarily accepting them, but at least acknowledging them.

In order to do that, we must condition ourselves and our minds daily to new challenges and to truly aim at making a positive impact in our communities and those around us. Sometimes we are the limit to our imaginations and abilities, whereas we should be the biggest supporter and motivator in our own lives. That means not being close-minded to learning, but instead allowing knowledge of all sorts to cross your path on a daily basis. I find it very useful sometimes to take a break from the hectic trials of life and to write about the things I notice daily—the stories I hear and the people I meet—and through these moments create a lesson learned from those experiences.

You will be surprised at what the little things in life can teach you about the world, about who you are and can become if you take time out to chart your life's purpose. This new fast-paced technology age has truly caused us to shy away from relaxation and personal time with ourselves. If you are not healthy or not taking care of yourself first, then there is no way you can make a grand and positive impact on the lives of others. Therefore, forget about the past, start afresh, and remember that your thoughts and imagination are the driving force in your quest for knowledge and good fortune.

## Yes We Can

A nation divided and a world in peril, how much could we possibly hope for?

*"We've been asked to pause for a reality check. We've been warned against offering the people of this nation false hope. But in the unlikely story that is America, there has never been anything false about hope."*
President Barack Obama

Hope—my life, your life, and this country were founded on a belief that we could do better than tyranny or a monarchy. Within all of us, we held the belief that we could build a nation that was as just and free as we hoped for. We may not have seen the light 20 years ago or 50 years ago, but through faith and hope we have discovered that we are more similar than we are different. Our melting pot of cultures, races, beliefs, and ideals rings from "coast to coast and from sea to shining sea."

Our nation was not built out of fear or lack of innovation, it was built on the belief that we would be a shining light for the entire world to see and believe in. And as we stand today, we have lost some of that glare and spark, but we should not be afraid or fear to correct our mistakes. America has never been fearful of the unknown and it has never been fearful to rise up in times of sorrow and darkness to provide a new way of hope and prosperity. There are three words that were vital to the foundation of America, vital to those who had no voices or rights, vital to making America a land of the free and home of the brave: Yes We Can.

We have never achieved anything in this country or in our own lives without the belief that it is possible, and that even though our sight may be jaded or near-sighted, deep down inside we believe and we know that anything is possible. If a nation can rise up for justice, if a nation can rise up against tyranny, if a nation can rise up against hate and disdain, we can rise up as one people, and one nation to "begin the next great Chapter in the American story with three words that will ring from coast to coast from sea to shining sea"-Yes We Can!

As a nation whose destiny lies in the hands of its people and not of its government, it is our civic duty to fight for those who have no voice, who have no rights and no ability to hope, right here in our own country. A generation of young people is rising up, fighting for, and believing again that we can bring about change in this country, where our voices can be heard. With a president who believes in us and believes in our ability to bring about positive social change, anything is possible. How many times have we as young people been told we are not capable of doing something? That we should put our trust in those with experience, that we should wait our turn? That we are not ready?

We are ready! We can bring about a nation that listens to its citizens, which fights for a greater future than what is in front of us, and in the words of President John F. Kennedy, *"ask not what your country can do for you—ask what you can do for your country."* In the story of America and its history, how likely is it for a black child to go to college with students that are white, international, and of all creeds and colors? Our past told us that women could not vote and hold positions of power. How likely was it for a woman and black man to be leading candidates for President of the United States? This is our America, an America that has been changed and molded, not by the mere signing of laws or power of the presidency, but through the voices and demands of the people.

Change can only come about if someone stands up for justice, stands up for freedom, stands up for hope! Without our voices, there is no change and there is no hope. When one stands, another follows, then another, and then a few hundred, and then a couple thousand, and then a nation! Our nation must no longer follow the hollow drums of a few, but must follow the chorus of a nation. Ten years from now, twenty years from now, we will be a part of history, but what history will it be? Will it speak of a generation that stood for nothing, that fought for nothing, but only the mere pleasures of the present, rather than reaching for the prosperity of the future? I do not know about you, but I do not want to be a part of that history.

I want to be a part of a history that speaks of a generation that fought for the poor and mangled; the weak and the destitute, the young and the old, the hopeless and the hopeful. We can be that history, and we can be that hope.

(Parts of the U.S. Presidential candidate Barack Obama's New Hampshire primary speech are used in this writing)

## Adding Extra Jazz in Our Lives

Let us all be honest, sometimes we do things in life that are completely overrated, but in order to be successful and useful to the world, we have to play the game, such as high school and college. We all know that we probably could have read those books on our own and had the same outcome. However, there is something that comes out of the interaction, discussion, and support we get from others. Life is all about jumping into as many opportunities and adventures that provide positive and exciting outcomes. Sometimes we forget to take time out to relax as we are too busy trying to change the world or change other people. Before any of us can make a real difference, we have to put our lives on the right track.

We will not always succeed at everything, failure is a part of life as those are the characteristics that shape, mold, and grow us as human beings. Many of the world's most successful people talk of being patient, idealistic, and most importantly, determined in achieving their goals and successes in life. We should always be working towards what we can do better together as a people as we all share in the failures and successes of one another. A cure for cancer will not only help the person(s) who discovered the cure, but also millions of other people now and in the future. A new energy source will not just help the company that has discovered or developed it, but it well help consumers, our earth, and future generations.

Our innovative society has never backed down in the face of adversity, but has risen to new heights and new exciting ideas. As a way to cultivate our ideas and our minds, we must never forget to jazz up our lives by taking time out for ourselves. For many, that will mean exercising, playing their favorite musical instrument, writing, reading, or simply taking a nap everyday to rest the mind and body. Whatever your jazz is in life, take hold of it and do not let go. Do not allow yourself to be over-worked and overtaxed! Live an exciting and fulfilling life, work towards improving the lives of others, and truly open your mind and soul to new ideas and never forget your own values and the sacrifices others have made for us all.

### Defining Success

Success can be defined as wealth, power, happiness, family, friends, luck, hard work, or achieved goals. What exactly determines success in the 21st Century and what is the definition of success? Is it achieving a set goal? Making millions off a successful product or service? Is it going to college and living a great life with a family? Ultimately, success is defined by each individual. However, if you are aiming to have a successful life that is defined by how you change the environment around you, as an entrepreneur is concerned, how do you achieve that level of success that is noticed by society and be rewarded for it? For many who achieve success in the business world, a string of many actions precipitated fully fledged success. For instance, Bill

Gates credits the fact that he was able to have access to a computer when most citizens did not as a means for his future success. Imagine if Bill Gates never came into contact with a computer and what the world would look like today? Some people are able to truly change society as we know it based on their life experiences and connections.

If you look at other success stories in the entrepreneur world, success comes from a myriad of opportunities, luck, perseverance, dedication, and resources. I believe that everyone has a success vision within them, but most will never be tapped. They will never have the opportunities they need, the resources, the support, or the luck. Today success is so narrowly defined and cultivated, that for many, if you live outside of mainstream society and do not have the connections or education to progress and push your ideas, you may never be heard or seen. However, even if you feel left out of the process and unable to push through to the front, success can be achieved in practically all areas over time.

Simply start with a vision and truly think about how that vision can become real and create a positive impact on society. Read articles, books, magazines, and other success stories that correlate with your vision. Then you must begin to write out those thoughts and ideas—map out the pros and cons, mission, vision, overall strategy for success, and any other details that come to mind. And most importantly, talk to close friends and relatives that can provide encouragement and advice. The worst thing you can do is keep your vision bottled up.

You may end up meeting someone who can move you further down the path to success. It is also vital that you believe in your vision, because people know when you truly believe in your passion and are more willing to join your cause. Lastly, take risks and do not give up. Nothing was ever started and completed without some form of risk taking, whether you need to take out loans to start a venture or work an extra ten hours a week, whatever those risks are, ensure that they move you along in your quest for success and stay committed.

Success truly is what you make it and how far you are willing to go. Through your success, I hope you find the most ultimate goal of all: happiness.

## Have Faith in Yourself

As I reminisced on the passing of the Liberal lion Ted Kennedy and all that he did for this country from Civil Rights to health care to education, I realized that he was truly a man of many ideals and a belief that government could truly be an equalizer and fighter for those with no voice or foundation. This was a man, who like most of us, was not perfect by any means. He had his demons, but overtime picked himself up and became a true model and shining light for those who needed a helping hand. In our day and age it is hard to find those stories of true and lasting faith in oneself, even in the darkest hour. Many people simply allow their worries and troubles to overtake their lives and never get back on the path to success.

Life is truly defined by our ability as humans to right the wrongs we witness, to fight for something greater than ourselves, and to consistently strive for purpose in all that we do. No one is perfect; however, each day should be a positive step towards fulfilling each of our own life stories—stories that will travel different paths, new dreams and goals, and hopefully one day that will cross with someone else who holds the same visions and passions as you do. Believing in oneself is about taking a bold stand to never dwell on the past, but to always live in the present and prepare for the future. There is nothing wrong with doubt, but never allow it to overpower the idea of hope and a promise that each and every day is a new day to fulfill your own individual destiny.

The future may be somewhat frightening for many especially with the loss of jobs, health care, and many wars; however, there is always hope for a better tomorrow. The idea that one day the sun will shine brighter, the sky will be bluer than the prettiest ocean, and our lives will be a beacon of opportunity and innovation for generations to come is the true American spirit.

## Empowering a Generation: Replicating Success and Building Self-Worth

Having spent over a year and some change in the nation's capitol, I have been disheartened with the quality of life and support that many residents of the district experience every single day, especially the horrid conditions our young people endure. The lives of many American youth intertwine with many citizens across oceans, villages, and cities that are impoverished, uneducated, dimensioned, and unheard. Their cries for help are ignored and their basic needs are unmet within their communities. For decades many of our leaders have outright ignored millions across this great nation who have been left behind. As we have seen in this current global economic crisis no one is left unscathed when our own greed and self-interest take hold over basic principles of ethics, humanity, and social responsibility.

The saddest part is when we choose to ignore the plight of those less fortunate and those most affected are the most vulnerable to start with: young people. Many people never realize that they are being treated as second-rate humans without such basic needs as shelter, clothing, food, health care, or even a good education. In the end we all suffer, as success and self-worth are seen as two commodities that many are not able to reach or even imagine. The idea that we can fail our young people day in and day out and not feel their pain or hear their cries for help is astonishing. In order for America and the world to truly rise from its own failures and unjust ways, we must begin to put people first. We must understand that this generation of young people will soon inherit this planet.

When I went into a Washington, DC Public School to perform a student audit, I was somewhat surprised at the lack of positive improvement, even though I had worked in a Washington, DC public school for a year and knew the failures of the education system here and the strides they were attempting to make. However, some classes that should have had at least twenty-five students in them had five or six; the other students were nowhere to be seen. As a matter of fact, some had only showed up once in a two or three week period. I was truly alarmed and saddened that somehow we had accepted this as the status quo. However, I also knew how badly schools, the local government, and parents in the region had failed to truly understand and provide for the many young people across the district. As I walked into every classroom, I had a chance to interact with the students, many of them wondering why this young employee from the Chancellor's Office was in their classroom and others not really caring one bit.

I was excited to see teachers teaching and students learning, albeit many slept at their desks or had an iPod in as the teacher taught, but this was what they were expected to do. Not many people praised them, believed in them, motivated them, supported them, or even cared about them. Many went home every single day to an empty house where they cared for their brothers and sisters. Their only lunch and dinner was what they had at school (which was not the healthiest of foods) or a quick stop to McDonalds because it was inexpensive and quick, especially when they were from a one parent home (mom worked two jobs). For many in DC and the nation, this is a cycle and recipe for failure and disaster. Not only do these young people live in social environments that breed violence, drugs, lack of innovation, etc., but they head to a neighborhood school that is an extension of that community. Instead of being a model for success, independence, hope, education, and constant learning, schools simply become just another place to act up, get in trouble, and learn absolutely nothing.

The question then remains how do we break this cycle? How do we instill within our young people that life can be successful, that their goals and visions for a better life can be realized, no matter what their past or present life is like. No matter the toughness of their path or lack thereof, anything is possible if they truly believe in themselves, put in the time to succeed, and never give up. Living a life of self-worth, happiness, and success is no easy task, especially with the negative forces surrounding many of these disadvantaged youth each and every day, but it is possible. There are some important ingredients to creating lasting self-worth and success in one's life, no matter what he or she has done in the past or what condition he or she lives in or how their school looks or how good his or her parents are. Each one of us has within us the ability to formulate and create a life of ultimate success and self-worth.

1) Faith—young people must have faith in themselves and their abilities to positively change their lives and the environment around them. It starts out with simply imagining a better home, a better life, a better neighborhood, and knowing that you can be a part of that vision and that hope.

2) Living with a purpose—I think for many young people, they simply do not see a purpose to this whole thing called life. They question their parents, they question their teachers, they question learning and, simply put—they question life. When you can wake up every single day with a reason for doing so, knowing a new day is another opportunity to succeed at your dreams and your visions, it truly becomes a miracle and the positive energy you put into that day will reap many benefits.

3) Innovative drive—once you have the purpose—excel at it, stay determined, and never give up. If you believe in your own innovative ideas and abilities, you cannot fail—at least not due to your own doing. The most disheartening way to fail is by your own hands. Do all in your power to succeed and surround yourself with positive/uplifting people who can help you on your path to success.

4) Individuality—it is important to be yourself—whatever that entails. Enjoy life to the fullest and know what you stand for—never compromise your beliefs and ethics. It is impossible to enact success and know your self-worth if you do not know you! Individuality also entails constant learning. Education is

not just during school or in college, but something you should always embrace and partake of all the days of your life.

5) Be the change—represent what you truly believe in and stand for! Give back to your community and others, knowing that by serving others you are serving the well-being of mankind. Spread your ideas and hopes so others can join your quest. Live the life you were meant to live. Everyone has a purpose and each person deserves to live a full and prosperous life.

Every young person can and should believe in him or herself in all that they do. They should also be provided the tools and resources necessary to succeed and to build self-worth. The problems America and the world face are too big to leave a whole generation left behind. My hope is that I will be able to spread this message through words and sound to as many young people as possible as a mentor, friend, and leader.

## Can You Change the World?

There is a point in all of our lives when we realize our potential and our ability to positively change the environment around us. But at what point do we act? When do we finally see that clear path and the epiphany that graces our inner thoughts? It is vital that we become empowered—that our souls and minds become awakened to our true calling. This awakening for many people occurs due to a negative experience or tragedy—our senses become awakened due to a loss of a job or close friend or family member.

The idea that life on this earth is not everlasting, that it is finite, should guide us. Others experience their own calling due to positive experiences, such as spiritual awakenings or life-changing conversations and opportunities that open up the mind and soul. Our time here is our opportunity to bring about real positive ideals and changes to the lives of others.

When we not only discover our purpose, but learn to love ourselves and others more holistically, we then realize the power within each of us. It is very easy for us to wait on someone else to live our dreams for us or to give us the golden ticket, however; our fear of the unknown and the risks involved with success should not be the ultimate decider in our own quests to discover who we are as individuals and what we are meant to accomplish in our lives and in the lives of others.

In a simple term: faith! Having faith to leap before looking, travel on the unknown path, and take the risks necessary to achieve important goals that may sometimes end in failure, and then our ability to get back up when down and to learn from our failures and the failures of others in our own quest to succeed, are all part of the defining cycle of life and success.

The idea that a young nun with only her faith in Jesus Christ could become one of the most prominent humanitarians ever is amazing. Winning the Nobel Peace Prize and helping thousands of impoverished and diseased people across the world find comfort and solace—this is a story of divine faith. Mother Teresa once said, *"The more you have, the more you are occupied, and the less you give. But the less you have, the freer you are. Poverty for us is a freedom."*

We can look at the story of a South African man for hope who was imprisoned for twenty seven years in a country that was a breeding ground for discrimination and apartheid. No one could have imagined then that he would rise up to lead a free South Africa into a new era of inclusiveness and diversity. Nelson Mandela showed that even in a man's darkest days he can rise up to take on new and daunting challenges that embroil a nation and a divided people. Nelson Mandela once said, *"I was not a messiah, but an ordinary man who had become a leader because of extraordinary circumstances."*

There are many stories of normal people doing extraordinary work that ultimately impacted thousands, if not millions of people. If you read and listen to their stories they all used their circumstances, whether negative or positive, to their advantage to bring about real change in society and the world in which we live today. The story of life for all of these individuals and our own lives are linked inextricably together. Through the discovery of our own purpose on this earth brings about a new identity and awakening in the lives of others.

Live your life to the fullest. Be inspired. Live your dreams and deepest wishes. Every success starts with an idea. Be creative and never give up!

- How can you change the world?
- What are your interests? What gets you excited?
- Take a personality/interest test.
- Write about your life and piece it together.
- Lose yourself in service to discover your purpose.
- If you are religious, pray and seek spiritual guidance.
- What lifelong goals or dreams do you wish to accomplish?
- Take some time off to meditate and relax your mind and soul.

## What Happens When You Lose Everything?

There are many times I think about what would happen in my life if I lost everything in terms of a job and a sense of financial security. Millions of people across this country are going through this experience every day. Many people that were making six-figure incomes and those who were middle-class Americans working every single day just to stay afloat during this economic tidal wave, have experienced dramatic loss. Anytime our nation goes through a recession, we do not quite know what it means to be jobless, poor, and without a sense of stability and opportunity until we have truly been there. However, I do like to put myself in the shoes of others by reading and learning about those who have lost everything, but somehow still manage to wake up every day with their pride and belief that a brighter day is before them.

I believe there are two responses that one can have when faced with the loss of a job and economic stability. The first option is to simply give up. Just think for a minute of being called into your boss' office, with the door shut as you walk in and the lights flickering just a little. "I'm sorry, but due to budget cuts your position is no longer needed, I'm so sorry." Your face is in an aura of shock, unable to truly compute and put into context what just happened. You come back to reality and start thinking about bills and debt, providing for yourself and your family if you have one, rent, health insurance, and all those things that you need to feel like a human. The response for many when dealt with this situation is to quit. When the pressure and stress combine around you, it may be too hard to overcome. This individual may apply for a couple of jobs here and there, but they simply do not have the will or motivation to push on and to plan for a new future.

Then there are those who leave the office that day, shed some tears, question their own ability to survive, and at the end of the day they pick their heads up, wipe their faces, and decide to see this life change as a new challenge to reinvent their own lives. They learn that they can live within their means and that there is a brighter tomorrow even when darkness is clouding their present. The ability of those who are faced with controversy and unknown challenges to rise above the fray and to become innovators in their own right is the definition of what America is truly about. Picking yourself up, living your life to the best of your ability, and adjusting to adverse circumstances to create a better future for yourself and those around you shows faith and strength.

Every challenge and success in each of our lives presents itself with unique opportunities and doors that we may never have seen or opened. We realize that we are not defined only by what we do or who we go out to eat with or what we buy, but by our own beliefs and ideals that for many of us encompasses faith, hope, innovation, and a zest for life itself. Using adversity to ones advantage is not always easy as the stress can be too much, the debt builds up, and the mortgage is no longer affordable—all of these things and more put stones and trees in our paths that we are tasked to overcome and navigate around to live out our own lives.

When you lose everything, life itself must seem to stop, but in reality, for many it is a new beginning with new opportunities to travel, be free from the stress and tension of working every single day, spend more time with family and friends, start that dream business, and live out life-long goals and dreams. Instead of quitting, those who choose option two use their own innate creative and entrepreneurial talents to make positive change, not only in their own lives, but in the lives of others. As our nation continues to face the effects of this recession and our economy slowly recovers, it is vital that each of us remembers that nothing is ever promised tomorrow and that everyday should be spent living out our goals and innermost dreams and making the world a better place.

**The Simple Life: What Path Will You Take?**

There are many days that I think about the simple life or the old fashion way of doing things. The idea that after high school comes college where I would meet my sweetheart and marry, land a good paying stable job, have amazing children, and do nothing to upend the sense of tranquility, independence, and self-gratification. I would choose not to get involved with politics, local community affairs, or concern myself with the issues of the world. While living in this simple life I would take a family vacation once a year and make sure my kids are happy and attain a great education. O what a magnificent picture I am conjuring up in my head right now: the simple life, I like to call it. What if I decided that my life would have taken a different path that was a little bumpier and uncharted that relied on faith, determination, and self-sacrifice?

There are no guarantees of success, happiness, or even a peaceful ending. But those risks could provide an amazing opportunity, a triumphant end I would say. I was raised by my parents to never give up, to follow my dreams, and most importantly, to have faith and never lose hope. It is when we believe in ourselves, even in the darkness of night, even when all seems worthless and empty, that we build fortitude and ultimate purpose. When we as a people seek out the plight of others to offer support, guidance, and healing, we learn more not just about ourselves, but about others.

The ultimate human emotion: love. Sometimes it is hardest to love ourselves even as we seek to love others. We look in the mirror and we look at our fallacies, our own transgressions, our imperfect behaviors and we seek forgiveness and understanding to better guide our paths. Once we can accept our own imperfections and work to improve them, only then can we seek out others in a quest to improve the world in which we live in—a truly imperfect world, one in which we are constantly bombarded with false hopes, violence, drugs, and what many would deem illogical behavior by our fellow peers. After all of these thoughts I then think to myself, "how am I going to fix this?" And then a quick, "O yeah, it is not just about me, it is about all of us!" How can each of us play a positive role in improving the earth and the world in which we all live and are an intricate part of? Yes, the world around us can beat us up pretty bad sometimes, it can damper the happiest of moods, destroy the will to succeed, and for many completely halt the dreams and ideals of a generation.

It would be very simple to just give up....
It would be very simple to tap out....
It would be very simple to say well, that was a good try....
It would be very simple to say I tried...
It would be very simple to say it's not affecting me...

O yes, how simple life would be if none of us played a role in the world's final outcome. How we treat one another is telling and indicative of our society at large. The troubles we face are many, the potential failures are infinite, but you know it only takes one success to lift up the spirits of one and to eventually reach many more to take risks, never give up, and dream big! The idea that life has a purpose and that we are all connected and called upon to reach out to one another in hopes of building a more fruitful and awe inspiring world around us is a journey worth discovering. This world will end one day as we are promised of this, but what will not end is the eternal quest for peace, hope, and prosperity in each and every soul that inhabits this earth. Let us think big and live lives worthy of a higher purpose and a higher calling, let us be fruitful in our endeavors and reach out to others, ultimately changing not only the world around us, but history itself. *"The past is strewn with the ruins of the empires of tyranny, and each is a monument not merely to man's blunders, but to his capacity to overcome them. We must meet the forces of hate with the power of love"*—Martin Luther King Jr.

## The Imperfect Reflection: How Education is Failing Our Children

From day one as kids we are taught to think a certain way, learn certain amounts of information in a particular day and school year, and that we can be anything we want to be. Except all of those adults (including some parents) forgot to tell us society has already reserved certain positions of power and hierarchy to a select few, while the rest of us are destined to a life of mediocrity and compliance—if we do not become awakened to tear down the status quo. The point in which we asked our teachers, "Why do we need to know this?" their response was simply "just do the work" or "you want to graduate don't you?"

The sad fact is even our teachers knew then that the education system in which we were learning in and they were teaching in, was simply a cultural phenomenon in which only a select few would make it out and truly make a difference, while the others labeled as "the slow kids, special education, non-honors" would be left with the dirty work. Quite frankly when I look back at this sort of divide in our society it is disgusting and leaves me wondering how will the rest of our future generations turn out in the midst of our quite standard educational system that still seems to be stuck in the 1970s? Are we so stuck to the point of no return? How do we reinvigorate a sub-par education system to match the idealism and creativity of a more open and diverse global society without disregarding the need for a strong national identity?

Those are just a few questions that we as a society must begin to answer sooner rather than later. In school I was always the one in class to question my teachers, my principal, and even my superintendent on why the system was the way it was. I never felt like it was working for the majority of young people, nor did I feel like it really stimulated the intellectual diversity within my classes. Clearly, we need students to understand the basics of math, reading, and language arts, which are all vital to building a strong learning core for other subjects; however, there was never much thought or attention to the developmental needs of young minds.

As kids our minds are like sponges and we learn quickly, we are willing to try new subjects and learn languages faster and are truly just beginning what seems like the greatest adventure of our lives. Little did we know, at some point the system would no longer cater to the creative and experiential minds of our youth. There are hundreds of amazing public schools across America that are excellent incubators of education reform and truly allow their students to take control of their own futures and creative landscapes. My hope is that we can learn from those successes and repeat them in other schools across the country.

We all want to be successful and a part of something greater than ourselves. There is a universal thought process in which we all have a vision in mind for how our lives will pan out, except for some reason we will not always reach that hopeful cloud in the sky. Even if as individuals we will not all attain our goals and dreams, we should each at least have that opportunity. Innovation and a society built on multi-national and cultural connections are truly the building blocks for a future that embraces the individual person and his or her identity to be self-sufficient and open. I have always believed that there is something for everyone, that life is not in vain, and if there is a problem to be solved, an invention to be created, a song to be written, a painting to be designed, or a dream to be lived, it is right here on this earth.

Our leaders must acknowledge that perfection should not be the definition of success nor should a single test or a horribly rigid systematic education system fraught with institutional fallacies of how children should be educated as a single entity, be the only options for learning. We need an educational system that embraces diversity, not just of color, but of ideas, thinking, and artistic abilities. We need teachers who are free to teach in a manner that embraces different learning styles and truly embraces a different generation of young people. We need an educational system that embraces technology and the ever expanding social network of our young people. And most importantly, we need an educational system that values trial and error that encourages students to try something they may not be entirely comfortable with, to give it their best shot, and no longer institutionally point our young people where we think they should be. We must let each student's own destiny be their guide to life and liberty.

I challenge every young person to step out of his or her comfort zone, to try something new, to always learn more and more, and to be open to new endeavors except mediocrity.

Live loud.

Enjoy friends and family.

Yearn for the mysteries of learning.

Explore new challenges and risk failure.

Give back to others, planting seeds of opportunity.

## The Promise of the Human Spirit

As I go about my day, sometimes I wonder if people realize that life is finite. Everything we own, create, build, design, mold etc. will at some point no longer be a part of us. What will last are the memories, our legacies, and the love we shared with others. The energy it takes for us to hate others, to destroy, and to tear down could be better used to build up and to shape a better planet for future generations. We live in a dangerous world where criminals and those who wish to take the lives of others are just as prevalent as those who seek to instill peace in a warring and desolate society. However, the cause of humanity and the awakening of our minds to create a more just and free society should always be our ultimate goal—even in the face of darkness, war, hate, destruction, and insecurity.

The human mind is the most powerful and creative resource of any creature on this earth. Our ability to reason, to see hope out of despair, to love those who we call our enemies, and to seek out new solutions to complex problems, make us truly different. Our own existence is proof that there is much more to this life than our own ephemeral actions. What we make of our time on this earth should evolve around improving the lives of others, building up communities, creating a sustainable society for future generations and ultimately leaving this planet better off than when we came. As our politics may divide us, we must not allow political ideology to define our aspirations as a people and a society to promote and create a brighter future for the next generation.

We live in tough times, quite drastic times actually, and we must not let our shortsighted views inflict permanent and long-term damage on the foundation in which all people are most greatly defined by: humanity. The idea and belief that we as a people are better off united than we are divided. Our freedom and justice are the defining equalizers of sustainable social progress. All people should be allowed to not just imagine their dreams, but to actively pursue them and ultimately, to live them. We should all seek out ways we can make the world a better place in our local communities, nationally, and globally. Even if it is just tutoring a child for thirty-five minutes, or building a community garden at a senior center, we can all pitch in to improve the lives of others and in the process remind ourselves of what we are truly here to do, which is to follow our dreams and create a lasting, positive social structure built on a foundation of humanity and sustainable social change for those who come after us.

## The Art of Happiness

There is something revealing and inspirational when we as individuals discover what truly makes us happy. Happiness with a career, friends, family, and life in general are goals we all strive for. For many, that moment is built up over time or discovered amazingly early. Happiness is truly an art that many of us spend years refining, orchestrating, creating, and designing. Sometimes it takes failure or disillusionment with the status quo before we realize what we are currently doing is not right for our psyche or the path to ultimate bliss and happiness. I like to think back to when I was a child and how much I enjoyed the quietness of my room and the outdoors— walking in the woods, listening to birds singing, fishing with my dad, and trying to dig for dinosaur bones. It did not take much as a child to bring out the enjoyment of life. However, as we all get older, some of those childhood memories of happiness fade away due to our newer, more demanding and somewhat trivial lifestyles that become part of a more diluted and expedient world.

We become more complacent with how things are, more subdued about life it-self, and ultimately aim more to fit in than to be different, to stand out from what the world says is right or wrong. Essentially we lose the prowess to engage our childish pleasures, to take risk, and to do what makes us happy; we placate the wants and demands of others to fit some path of conformity that we never anticipated abiding by. It reminds me of the kids who are afraid to color outside of the ap-proved lines, not because it creates some irreparable harm, but because the accepted ideology is that coloring inside the lines is more aesthetically pleasing, therefore to do otherwise is to deviate from societal norms. I would argue that we need more people to color outside of the lines, to challenge accepted norms and ideals, and to be innovative in their approaches to design and social change. We need to empower people to not just design their dreams, but to live them. The art of happiness is not meant for a select few nor is it created with barriers; it is meant for all of us to partake in and to discover and create.

It is easy to become jaded in a world filled with so much despair and unhappiness. Economic turmoil, war, tragic disasters, and much more blind out the positive outlooks in life. The world is truly what we make it, therefore the more people who decide to create their own form of happiness and share with others, the better world we can create together. We must inspire young people to not simply accept everything that they read, see, or are told, but to create their own rules and to live out their dreams without fear of being ridiculed and discouraged. Success is not just about the financial benefits or publicity; it is about doing what makes you happy in all facets of life. Waking up every day and being excited about your current circumstances and more excited about where you are headed is the ultimate hope of life on this earth. Live your life freely and without fear of being you, make a positive difference in the world, and do what makes you happy!

# 3

# LIVING WITH A PURPOSE AND MAKING A PLAN

*"I look forward to a great future for America - a future in which our country will match its military strength with our moral restraint, its wealth with our wisdom, its power with our purpose."*
-President John F. Kennedy

Through diligence, patience, and a spirit of determination one can achieve anything he or she sets his or her mind and heart to. Once you have faith in yourself, the next step is to understand the underlying purpose for which you exist on this earth. Why are you here? What is your calling? And how exactly do you get there? This section will seek to lay out the importance of living with purpose and how everyday should be a step towards achieving ones goals and visions for life. With the right mindset, you will then be ready to create and implement your own plan for success and happiness.

A)  What is Purpose?
B)  Discovering Your Purpose.
C)  Creating a Plan.
D)  Living your life's mission.

**What Are You Here For: Discovering Your Purpose and Succeeding!**

Every day I am constantly looking at society and the world around us. The issues that shape our daily beliefs, ideas, visions, and everything from education to health care to drugs. What makes the human mind tick and the way we think about every-thing? All these things are as complex as the development of an affordable hydrogen powered vehicle. It is amazing to think about how complex humans truly are in life. We all hold so many deep and personal beliefs and opinions about almost everything! We are shaped and molded not only by our individual experiences, but from experiences that we see daily within our families, friendships, on the news, or by what we see and read in newspapers, magazines, and on the streets. Some of us are passionate about ending hunger, while others are fighting for the environment.

We all have some deep and strong personal visions on how we see the world and what we as humans can do to improve it and keep it healthy and strong. For me, life is all about having a positive impact in the lives of others, particularly those who are less fortunate and are unable to fight for themselves. I feel very strongly about inner city schools and communities, mainly because that is where my family grew up and moved away from. I want other young people to have the same chance I had in life to be successful in all that they do. Life is not only about knowing what we stand for and fighting for those issues, but also about knowing whom we are and discovering our innermost thoughts and feelings. Because once we are able to do that, we can become a new light of hope and justice for the world.

We become more confident, self-reliant, and faithful in our mission on this Earth. No one person is on this Earth without a purpose and reason for living. Once we find our purpose, we can become visionaries of new ideas and thinking. Some people I consider visionaries are Colin Powell, Oprah, Martin Luther King Jr., Bill Gates, and Mark Zuckerberg. All of them figured out their purpose in life, pursued it greatly, worked hard, and made a positive difference in their respective fields. Never be afraid to just open your eyes, ears, heart, and soul to the world around you, because you never know what you might discover deep within yourself!

### Living A Successful Life and Making Dreams Come True!

Waking up every day and working towards goals and ideas define your potential for achievement. It is no good to set low, measly goals for achieving, it is much more exciting and interesting to set large goals that will help to shape and mold the decisions you continuously make on a daily basis in preparation to reach your ultimate destiny. Every day should be lived in an attempt to reach that goal of truth. Everyone is capable of being the person they want to be. It takes hard work, dedication, goal-setting, and a will to succeed, but in the end, life will be much better and pleasing. Every young person should be provided the resources and lessons to help them discover what their true talents and gifts are in life. Our society should be one of dreamers and doers, rather than laid back, non-achievers.

Every day we should all be counting our blessings in life and thankful for what we have been given in way of talents and gifts to leave our mark on the world. Every day is a new day...a day of new chances and opportunities of growth, change, and unlimited potential. We just have to be willing to take hold of those great chances of opportunity we have been given. Be a visionary optimist for today and till the end of your life and I promise you, success is just right around the corner. Every person, particularly young people has the power within them to be beacons of hope and justice to all people. The youth of today's generation are the future leaders of tomorrow, the future shakers and movers of our society. We can either choose to run away from those duties or confront them head on with excitement, ingenuity, and a new perspective on life. Never give up in all that you do and your dreams will come true!

## Reinventing the Human in You

We have all heard about the importance of "re-inventing the wheel" and "thinking outside the box" in terms of innovation. It is just as essential that we continue to re-invent and re-invigorate ourselves as human beings. A very important aspect of maturing and growing is that we should all constantly be learning from our mistakes, listening to others more often, and taking time off to truly understand our purpose and reason for living on this earth. I am always looking for new ways to make my life more meaningful and interesting, because if I do not, I would probably go crazy.

We cannot allow ourselves to become complacent with the rigors of everyday life, instead we must continuously comb through our brains, hearts, souls, and lives to strengthen our inner being and our dreams for life. There is nothing wrong with changing paths, trying new things, and re-inventing the human in you. For many of us, that may be rediscovering our spirituality, taking yoga classes, reading more, or simply taking a break out of each day to meditate with our favorite music. Whatever that "re-invention" is for you, do not be afraid to do it regularly and share it with others. Many people burn themselves out by worrying about every little issue, instead of taking life's problems in strides. I am a very staunch believer in the idea that everything happens for a reason and eventually all things will work themselves out one way or another.

Living a life of inspiration and idealism is not always easy, but I promise you it is a lot more fun than living a life of despair and worrying. Whatever your problems may be or your lack of enthusiasm for life is, never forget that life will get better. You must be willing to place your ideas and hopes on the line, because no one ever succeeds without trying. My high school math teacher and student government adviser, Mrs. Zobel, wrote to me once—*"May Your Dreams Take You Far!"* Use these words and dream big!

## Individuality

> *"The really valuable thing in the pageant of human life seems to me not the State but the creative, sentient individual, the personality; it alone creates the noble and the sublime."*
> -Albert Einstein

The source of human inspiration can be defined as finding our individual niche and path to life—fulfilling our hopes and dreams and ultimately finding out who we are. Life is all about self-discovery—your own individuality and thrust for knowledge. I admire creations such as Facebook, because they are a part of that process. When I scan my friends Facebook profiles, they are all so different—each conveying a myriad of thoughts, ideas, and interests on life, culture, and creativity, not just as one individual, but as a generation.

Generation Y is constantly searching for answers to simple and complex problems, and railing against the status quo. As a member of Generation Y, we do not always understand what we are doing or even why we are doing it, but if it gets us from point A to point B, then so be it. Some choose harder, longer and more difficult paths to achieving their ultimate goals and visions, but nonetheless, life is not an easy path to begin with. We are constantly changing, thinking, growing, and finding.

Just look back at where you were a year or two ago—I am sure you can point out a number of differences about your life then and now. It may be the people you associate with that are different, or habits you have kicked or maybe even picked up, your outlook on life, your beliefs, etc. And that is totally fine—life would be very boring if we all stayed the same and did everything the same. Looking towards the future requires constant monitoring and evaluation of our short and long term goals and tweaking those goals according to our life adjustments.

Forever remembering where you come from, becoming independent and charting your own life map are the highlights of being an individual. So find your niche and forever conquer your quest for knowledge and enjoyment.

## Destiny

It is said that in life, success is what we make it and that we determine our own dreams and visions for our own futures. However, for many people that is hard to believe. They may have lost their home due to foreclosure or had a messy divorce with huge attorney fees or lost their scholarship in college due to a bad semester. People going through tough times generally do not see themselves to blame for their predicament as it becomes too easy and comforting to find another entity or reason to find fault for one's own failures. That is not to say that at times in our own lives our failures may have been caused by no fault of our own. However, to a certain degree we are truly in control of our own destinies.

We decide how far we want to push ourselves, who we want to become friends with, the level of education we strive to attain, the information that we place in our minds, and so forth. Throughout my life I have been pretty successful for my age and achieved so many of my goals such as writing a book, attending college, meeting inspiring leaders, holding numerous leadership positions, committing to national service, having great friends and family, and so forth—I have so much to be thankful for, I have been truly blessed.

Throughout history the world has seen an amazing flurry of spiritual and creative individuals ranging from Jesus to Gandhi to Buddha and so forth. These individuals and many others saw life as a means to improve not only their own conditions, but the plight of others. Through helping ones neighbor, giving back to their communities, and living life in the utmost positive way, this would in turn empower each individual and those around them to constantly seek success and happiness. Spiritual teachings in most religions teach the core foundations of loving thy neighbor, reaping what you sow, and positive thinking as a means to success and happiness among other principles. However, most of us do not live out those core values on a daily basis and do not see those as a means to accomplish anything. That is not to say that we have not tried or that we do not believe in those ideals, however we get so busy and tied up with the problems of the world and living our own lives trying to survive, that we forget why we are truly here.

We constantly hear older adults tell stories of how fast life blew by and many have regrets, while some do not. I am sure you all have had older adults in your life that are pleasantly happy with the way things turned out and truly love living and have reaped the success of true happiness and spiritual growth; but then there are those who are bitter, angry, and beholden to their own failures and lack of successful living, that they fail to truly recognize that they themselves held the most powerful sway in determining where they are today. I believe, as I have begun to learn and grow as a human being, that there are some very core values and ideals that we should all attempt to live out and with that will cause success in all realms of your life: career, finances, spiritual growth, love, etc.

First and foremost you must love yourself and believe in your own abilities and talents. For many of us, it is easy to try and solve other people's problems and jump in when we are not needed, that we forget to check ourselves in the mirror to rid ourselves of our own stains. If you do not love yourself, for whatever reason, it is quite impossible to love another person or even life in general. If you constantly look down on yourself, criticize yourself, and never attempt to make something of yourself then what can you do to become more positive? And if you are at that stage in your life now you must begin to figure out who you are and what your own abilities and talents are in relation to the world around you. Ask yourself, how can I make a difference? What are my goals and aspirations in my life? And how can they be achieved? No one will or can believe in you, if you cannot first believe in yourself.

As a kid growing up, my mom would always tell me how grateful she was that I was her son and how she knew I would grow up to do great things and to help people. As a kid hearing that from your mother you simply nod and smile, as you do not fully grasp the concept of such outward and futuristic thinking. However, as with most things, mother was right. I love helping people and putting a smile on people's faces, whether you are a friend or a simple stranger. Throughout high school I mentored others, volunteered, and always did my best to ensure other people were happy and successful. Those values for life truly came from my parents and their view of the world—that even when things are at their worst, there is no excuse to simply give up and stop giving back to others in need. In high school I had the opportunity to serve as class-president all four years and student body vice-president and president.

I was the jack of all trades, always aspiring to make a difference for my class-mates and to create a better school for future generations. As a kid, my siblings always taught me to set goals, post them in a visible area, and strive towards those goals every day, never looking back, and never giving up. I even had the opportunity to do an interview on the one year anniversary of 9/11 with Nippon TV, one of the largest TV networks in Japan, as they visited only a handful of young people across the world for a special that aired in Japan with the perspective of how 9/11 impacted young people around the world. I wrote constantly online and on paper, about issues that I felt were important such as education, health care, terrorism, youth empowerment, and so much more, and later got my own column in my town's newspaper, the Nassau County Record—albeit I only got paid thirty dollars per article (four to five articles a month), it was an awesome experience and fulfilled one of my dreams of becoming a writer. That dream later culminated in me getting a publishing deal for all my newspaper columns in a book entitled *"Writings from a Teenage Mind."*

I truly loved everything that I experienced throughout high school and the successes I had, but they did not come easy. It took hard work, dedication, faith, and most importantly, a vision. A vision that even as a young kid I could do anything I put my mind to—that my own thoughts controlled my own destiny. I felt that every success I had as a kid would lead to greater things and bigger successes later on in life. When I packed up for college, I was excited and nervous at the same time. Coming from a small, rural town of less than 5,000 people and moving into a downtown city was quite a change. However, it did not take long for me to find my avenues for success. I got involved with student government, actually losing my first run for office for freshman congress by one-fourth of a vote and yes, they did have a recount! I felt quite devastated to say the least and thought I would never run for anything again and would simply just give up. Well, I tried that and it was quite depressing to say the least as I stayed in my dorm room, did not venture out much with my fellow peers, and thought I would do better by not doing anything.

I ended up joining the campus programming board where we planned all of the on campus events from speakers to comedians to off-campus trips. I served as stage-shows chair and had the opportunity to plan, coordinate, and book some amazing acts to come to our campus. I felt back at home with myself and my talents. I loved my classes, my friends, and life was very good. But, if you know me well, I love to dabble in tons of activities, so I could not resist the temptation to get back into student government—with politics and serving others being my first love, it was hard not to. I gathered up my determination and energy and decided I would run for vice-president of student government when I was a junior. All I could think about was when I lost my freshman year and how I felt completely let down, but I knew that If I believed in myself and gave it my all, success and victory would occur. After the votes had been tallied, I waited for that call to come from the current student government president to let me know the news. As my phone ringed, I knew it was the president and she asked me how I was doing, I said great of course, and she said congratulations, you are the new student government vice-president! I was completely elated and excited, and started hugging everyone around me.

That year was great as we increased communication with the university senior staff, developed more leadership programming and increased the events sponsored by student government, as well as passed an updated constitution. I was extremely proud, although I always thought we could have done more and that always stuck with me up until my senior year of college. I decided not to run for president as I needed a break and felt compelled to jump back to the campus programming board where I served as vice-president my senior year and oversaw our budget and board members. I always felt this certain bond and purpose with ensuring students were greatly entertained!

Even with all of these amazing opportunities I needed more, so I joined a fraternity—Sigma Phi Epsilon. I was never the "frat" guy and never thought I would ever be compelled to join a "frat". However, once I met my soon to be brothers and learned about the personal growth and leadership aspects of joining, I became really intrigued and excited. The first thing I noticed was that Sig Ep does not use the word "frat", as it is considered detrimental to the values we live by: virtue, diligence, and brotherly love. Sig Ep is a fraternity, and although we loved to have fun and party, it was the ability to learn and grow from guys much older than I who had achieved many awesome accomplishments in life that meant so much to me. The battles and discussions that go on in a fraternity are special and you cannot recreate them anywhere else. I was elected chaplain of the fraternity my junior year, which was a big deal and a huge responsibility. My brothers had faith in my ability to bring the chapter together and fight for our rights. I began right away with the re-writing of our fraternity by-laws, which had not been updated in a while. I worked overtime and diligently with my board to ensure we updated the rules and regulations of the fraternity that fit our way of thinking and responsibilities as an organization. When we passed the new by-laws I was relieved, as it took a lot of hard work and motivation. Serving as chaplain was a very gratifying opportunity, as I had to constantly deal with situations involving disputes between brothers, the executive board, campus rule violations, and so forth; however, it made me a better person and I grew greatly in that position as a brother and a person.

While in college I also had the honor to participate in two alternative spring breaks, helping to rebuild hurricane stricken regions in Mississippi and New Orleans. Both were truly eye opening and amazing experiences that reinforced my belief in the strength and resilience of hard working Americans. Regardless of their predicament or hardships, the people of these two amazing places were willing to rebuild and forgive and even through their anger and loss, they had hope for a better tomorrow. Many lost homes, their family portraits and memories, and most important, many lost loved ones. How could these people who had lost so much and had so little still be so loving and caring? Simply put, they had a choice, as they had faced death once. Would they be bitter and live to die? Or live again to make their lives better? The second option was the prevailing answer from the people of the Gulf Coast.

They rebuilt their homes, businesses, and lives from scratch all over again. I could see the sweat and tears in the eyes of many of the residents as they retold their stories, their journeys, and hardships. One lady my group had a chance to meet at a gas station in New Orleans expressed her outrage at the lack of response from the government during the hurricane and up to that point. Thousands still lived in mobile FEMA trailers and had nowhere else to go. Another lady we met on the side of the street while we were painting an elderly lady's home, told us stories of families on roofs, many crying for help, some surviving, others dying.

I was truly heart stricken. Even after these tragic and heart-wrenching stories, they always ended with a story of hope, prayer, and a belief that the sun would be brighter on the other side. Many knew they had beaten the odds and stared death in its eye: why should they simply give up now? Life has many ups and downs and many set-backs; however, we should never use that as an excuse to quit. Instead we should use that opportunity of turmoil to change our own lives and environment around us to start anew and work to better not only the environment around us, but the world in general. The people I met in Mississippi and New Orleans taught me the importance of forgiveness, hard work, dedication, and an unyielding strength to prevail in the face of adversity.

After college I knew that I wanted to do something powerful, inspiring, and life-changing, so I joined City Year, a national non-profit devoted to mentoring and teaching children in our inner cities, among other activities, such as community service and HIV/Aids education. It was not so much about being a part of the organization itself that shaped me today as a person and an idealist, but the people I met and worked with every day, from the children to my co-workers to the people I met in the streets or on the metro. They inspired me to not give up, to dream big, and to truly fight for the social well-being of our present and our future. Giving back to those who have less is one of the most amazing and nurturing feelings one can attain.

The reason I bring up these stories is because these are times and moments in my life that have shaped me to be the person I am today. We all have these stories and they are vital in each of our quests to mature and grow as change-seekers. They help put life in perspective and to set us on a course for our own successes and even some failures. It is always important to learn from both success and failure, as they help you make adjustments in your own life and make the path to success and happiness just a little bit easier.

Secondly, loving thy neighbor is a core value. That does not mean you need to bring a box of chocolate to every neighbor close to you, but this is much bigger. Seeing the world around you, opening your eyes to different perspectives, and really attempting to be a positive influence to those you come in contact with is vital for happiness and long-term success. The way you treat other people reflects wholly on your own values and quest for a positive life. You would be surprised how people can pick up on the slightest change in facial/body movements, voice, etc. You never know who you may be standing next to or communicating with. People know when you are being fake, rude, or lying and it is a complete turn-off. Once you are confident with yourself, others will notice and they will feed off your positive energy and gravitate towards you. My parents raised my siblings and me to be respectful, not only to those who are respectful to us, but also to those who look down on us. Express a positive attitude and smile, regardless how others treat you, because at the end of the day you will prosper.

One day while riding on the metro in my full City Year uniform, which you could not miss by the way (huge red jacket with our logo, khaki pants, timberland boots, beanie, and gloves), a gentlemen asked what I did. It was early in the morning and normally I sort of just give our fifteen second elevator speech and that is it, however, I talked more and he was very intrigued about the City Year program (mentoring inner-city youth, volunteering) and he asked me what I planned on doing after City Year when my service year was up. I told him I wanted to work in government and go to graduate school in a couple of years and we chatted about life in general for a couple of minutes. Soon he started reaching in his briefcase and handed me his business card and told me to e-mail him my resume so he could help me potentially find employment once my service year was up, so I said awesome and I looked down at his business card and he was the Deputy Chief Security Officer at the Executive Office of the President! I said wow to myself, he could really help me out, so I made it a point to shake his hand before he got off the metro train and I e-mailed him my resume right away. These are the type of things that happen when you treat each person you meet with respect and kindness. You never know who is around you or what they could offer you.

Thirdly, you must search for your own success. Now this may be easy for others, however, there are many people who simply do nothing. They hope and wish for things, but they actually never go out and find success or happiness. They simply believe it will fall into their lap from the skies above. Nothing comes easy in life as there will be many ups and downs, happiness and sadness, trials and tribulations; however, your quest and search for the truth and for your own success should be never ending and all encompassing. Take some time to really map out your future and live life daily towards reaching those goals. There are many who refuse to set their sights on anything other than what is in front of them, what they can physically see and touch. And that, my friend, will not bring you very much. Sure it will help deal with your most immediate needs and wants, but you will never grow and achieve ultimate success and happiness if that is how you live on a daily basis.

You must have faith not only in your own abilities to achieve success, but faith in a spiritual force as well, whatever that entity may be for you. If you want to be a star football player, but never actually play football, work out, try out, eat healthy, etc., then chances are it will never happen. You have to want it more than the next person, believe in your own abilities and strengths and fight for it. If you want a promotion at your job you are not going to belittle your co-workers, show up late to work daily, or turn in late reports. You are going to come in early, stay late, have a glass of wine or a couple beers with your boss, do amazing work, tutor and mentor others, etc. In order to achieve ultimate success you have to search for it and make it happen.

With this proposition you must also work towards the future. It is important to live in the present; obviously you need to pay bills, provide food for yourself and so forth. However, to simply live in the shadow of your footsteps is not too promising or exciting. You need to stretch your imagination and truly believe that there are greater opportunities for you in life, that your potential is not yet realized and that there is a greater plan for you. For many, it is hard to live in both the present and the future, especially with the economic downturn, wars around us, disease, etc. Nevertheless, it is a vital must for you to achieve long-term success and happiness. I truly believe that every individual is capable of achieving anything he or she puts his or her mind to, work towards, and believes in. Just try it out once or twice and I promise you, you will be pleasantly surprised.

One weekend I was in dire need of some extra cash to help pay my part of the rent. I was really distraught at first and did not know where I was going to get the money from as the deadline was quickly approaching. As I kept devising ways to make money to pay my part of the rent, something clicked in my head and said "Josh, when have you ever just quit and stopped believing?" I immediately started searching online for random part-time jobs and I found approximately three or four and e-mailed the individuals. This was all done on a Monday or Tuesday and I needed the funds by the end of the weekend. Every day came by with no calls, but I knew I had tried, searched, believed, and did everything I was supposed to do, so now all I could do was wait. I woke up that Thursday morning sad to put it plainly, because I had no calls, but within a matter of time a lady called me by the name of Ms. Karen, asking if I was still available to work for her and her husband for the weekend. I jumped at the offer and woke up early that Friday morning to head to the metro, where they would then pick me up at a later metro stop. I was so relieved and my beliefs and dedication to achieving that goal were vindicated.

As I stepped into her car, she smiled and we exchanged greetings and we started to have some small talk about me, where I went to school, where I lived, what I was doing here in the DC area, and so forth. The first thing I noticed about Ms. Karen was her sense of hospitality and wholesomeness and I would not be disappointed. When we arrived at her home, I met her husband, Kevin, and they put me to work right away. Ms. Karen and Kevin was an older couple, both still working full-time. They were very smart, funny, and kind of hip, to say the least, for their age. However, they did not have much time or energy to do a lot of things they had neglected in and around their home such as cleaning out the garage and throwing old food away from the pantry. Ms. Karen was a cancer survivor and also needed knee surgery, so she was not able to lift things, exert force, or move around too much, which left her unable to do very simple tasks most people take for granted, such as reaching up to grab a plate or washing dishes. Her husband, Kevin, was a very funny and intelligent character. He had back problems, but was unwilling to let that stop him from keeping up with me. His wife pleaded for him to tone it down as she yelped "I would rather have a husband with a bad back, then a dead one," I found that odd and funny at the same time.

I was not only making a little money, but I was helping a couple who truly needed it. I worked with them for two days and I learned so much from them. First, I learned about the art of giving and joy. They truly enjoyed one another, their community, friends, and family. When I was helping Kevin clean out the garage, he told me how the neighbors loved their dog Starsky, a pretty big dog, but very gentle and playful. A couple of hours later, a few kids came up on their scooters and asked him if they could play with Starsky and he did not hesitate. He climbed down from the ladder he was on and went inside and let Starsky run free with the kids. I could just see the joy and happiness not just on the kids faces, but Kevin's as well. I stood there smiling and truly admiring how friendly both Kevin and Karen were.

Kevin and I talked about baseball, football, fishing, hunting, and his own hopes and dreams for when he retired. He hoped to live up in Pennsylvania close to a couple of lakes so he could go fishing more (he formerly owned a fishing supply store with his brother) and kayaking. He also enjoyed camping and said his big dream would be to work at Yellowstone for a year hiking and really enjoying nature and the beauty of the earth.

It was so amazing to be around someone much older than me who had such aspiring goals and dreams, and I knew that he was serious and they would come true. I kept telling myself if he can do it, even with his back problems and all the things that creep along as we get older, then why should a youngster like me or anyone for that matter, give up or not set life goals? His wife, Karen, was also a really inspiring individual. She talked about the amount of energy they put into their one child, who had emotional problems, and how that had slowed them down some and kept them from truly living their full potential.

However, they loved their daughter dearly and would do anything in their power to ensure she succeeded and lived a wonderful life. Karen wanted that year to be a new and refreshing year for her family—cleaning the house, going to church more, and so forth. As we sorted Christmas decorations, clothes, and everything else imaginable, she wanted to give everything to charity they could, so we placed all of those items in the back of Kevin's truck, and took them to Goodwill. Her plan was to donate items in their home they did not need at least once a week. This was such a simple goal that most of us never consider—old clothes and shoes that are never worn, childhood toys kept in the attic, and so forth—things that could enlighten a whole new person or a new family, while at the same time allowing us to give back to others.

She always talked about others positively and how they loved helping other people. Kevin was a member of numerous non-profit organizations and so was she. They gave from their heart dearly and were truly blessed and loved life. As we continued to sort, pack, and clean, the phone rang and Ms. Karen thought it was going to be the Girl Scouts asking if they wanted to purchase cookies, however, it was her best friend! She beamed with joy, as I am sure their schedule did not allow them much time to spend with others regularly, as she told me they barely ventured out from their home, except for work.

I was upstairs coming down and I could hear her beaming with joy about this young man who was in her home brightening them up, helping with everything, a gentlemen, intelligent, and friendly—and behold, she was talking about me! As I came all the way down the stairs she kept telling her friend, as she was laughing and smiling, how great a worker and joy I was to have around and recommended that if she needed any help around the house to call me. I could not comprehend how these people were so amazingly special and loving.

Not too long after that, the doorbell rang and Starsky ran down stairs waiting to greet the visitors, as he did with me. Kevin opened the door and it was the Girl Scouts selling cookies. Ah, I thought to myself, Ms. Karen was right, here they are. Kevin was delighted and responded gladly, "yes, we'd love to buy some cookies", with the biggest smile on his face. As he came back in after buying some cookies, the homemade pizza was ready that he cooked for us, so we all sat down at the kitchen table.

He proceeded to tell me how the young lady at the door instructed him how to fill out the paperwork to buy cookies and he said it was funny, "because he had bought cookies numerous times and was a veteran buyer." He bought three boxes that day and his wife jumped in and asked him "not to buy too many, as they had to make sure they bought some from the other girls that would come to their door!"

Kevin was the cook in the house and Ms. Karen professed her lack of cooking skills. I could tell that Kevin saw cooking as a creative and therapeutic activity. The first day I worked six hours and was supposed to get paid ten dollars an hour, which should have been sixty dollars for the day. However, as we rode to the bank as the sky darkened, he handed me eighty dollars and asked if that was enough. All I could say was thank you over and over again, as they knew I was in need of extra cash.

On the last day, as I finished cleaning out their pantry, I asked Mrs. Karen when she wanted me to come in on Sunday, which would have been a short day as I had church to attend and they had work on Monday. However, she explained how drained both she and her husband were from the two days of work around the house and that they needed to prepare for work on Monday. I completely understood and told her how much I enjoyed their hospitality and would love to come back anytime and she obliged, telling me how great it was to have me there and how much she enjoyed me around the house. Once again I worked six hours, so sixty dollars should have been my pay that day. As I hopped in their car she handed me a hundred dollar bill, and once again asked me if that was enough to help with everything. I was shell-shocked and amazed and said thank you over and over again and she looked me in the eyes and said "Josh, if you ever feel like you are in another bind like this and need money, do not hesitate and call us, I'm sure we can find you some work to do."

I was ecstatic to say the least, here I had met this couple I had never known and within two days they had become really great friends and role models. They were giving, loving, caring, and hospitable and loved life all at the same time and, most importantly, they treated people like they wanted to be treated. I truly believe that we meet certain people in our lives for a reason and purpose. We may not discover that reason at that exact moment or even days or weeks later, but at some point we do. Each person in our lives, whether he or she is there long-term or in passing, provides some form of energy and/or assistance to us that is either positive or negative. The goal is to be around those who are positive. Those individuals who are positive will assist you in your own growth and maturity; they will challenge you to succeed and to reach further than you ever have before. And most importantly, they will challenge you to think differently, not just about your own life, but the world around you.

How can you change the world? What is your purpose? Who are you and why are you here? These questions are constantly running through my head and they should be in yours as well. Life is a challenge, but it should not be a hindrance. You have to consistently evaluate those who are surrounding you, the decisions you are making about your life, your goals present and future, and so forth. Once you answer these questions, you will grow in your own shoes and lighten your path to success and happiness. Everyone has a story to tell about their life. What is your story? What are

your hopes and dreams; your passions, worries and frustrations? And most importantly, how will you succeed? How will you change your life course to be more positive,
lively, and successful? This is your life, so do something to change the world!

Life is truly what we design it to be. The talent is set, so the only question that
remains is are you going to get on the right path and stay the course. No one is
perfect and everyone makes mistakes, but the goal is to minimize those areas of
failure and to reach for opportunity and happiness in all areas of your life. Each of
us has the power to make it or break it, to take hold of it or to release it, to live or to
die. The people we meet, the challenges we face, for good or for worse, are a part of
who we are and who we are going to be. Shall we live in our own past transgressions
which hold us down? Or shall we reach out to the hopes and dreams of the future.
Faith, love, happiness, creativity, idealism, hope, success, and sharing your own
positive energy and zest for knowledge and life with others, are all abiding faiths and
virtues we should each carry with us at every moment and with every experience.

Success is not easy by any stretch of the imagination, but for any of you who
doubt your own abilities to bring about positive change, look at those around you
who have succeeded, who live abundantly, spiritually, thankfully, happily, joyfully,
positively, and successfully as a road map for your own life. A lot of times the things
closest to us, like our friends, family, associates, and even strangers hold the key to
opening us up to a whole new world. A world that is better than the violence on the
streets, the destruction of war, the hate around us, the impatience of everyday living,
and the negativity of our culture and way of living. I guarantee you a better life
awaits. People like Mrs. Karen and Kevin who still held their hopes and dreams, who
still believed in a better world, and not just believed, but lived it with pride. The key
is to live life to the fullest, knowing that every passing day could be your last, making
every moment count, and realizing that every word you say has an impact, every goal
you set can change the world, and that you control your own destiny. Think power-
fully, build creatively, and live positively!

### Living with a Purpose and Making a Plan

Our country and world face many unique challenges ranging from global warming to
economic despair to the need for cleaner energy. However, there is still much hope and
opportunity for those who are willing to live life with a purpose and calling. Many
people see having a purpose as simply a business model; however, it very much is a life

model as well. The idea that everything we do and engage in is driven by a core ideal and passion is one in which will lead to great and positive experiences and successes.

When you evaluate new opportunities and know what your core purpose in life is and what makes you truly happy, it will be very easy for you to say yes or no and forget about saying maybe. For instance, I have many passions in life such as education reform, inspiring young people, and challenging others to see life holistically as a means to bringing true and lasting social change. Whenever I get involved with a new project or even when I am making new friends or searching for a job, those are the things that stand out for me. Will that new job help me achieve those objectives? Will that new friend be a positive impact on my life and ideals?

It truly makes life easier and the decisions I make less daunting. I believe we all have a purpose on this Earth, although it may not always be apparent or come easy, it is always there within each of us waiting to be tapped, explored, and utilized to make the world a better place. We can all be idealistic visionaries for a better tomorrow— never losing sight of the present in our quest for future greatness. You should always ask yourself what mark you want to leave on the world. What is your point of existence? How can you bring about real and lasting social change? Take some time out of your busy day to write out your gifts, goals, passions, and what makes you happy to determine your purpose in life. I'm sure once you do that you will discover what truly inspires and drives you every single day. Living with a purpose relaxes you, makes life easier, more exciting, and meaningful. Go create something! Be your own inspiration and seek life goals that make you happy!

## Creating and Measuring Success

All successful organizations and companies both profit and non-profit, do a great job of not only developing their employees and overall goals, but also at designing and measuring the success of programs. It is very easy to design a program or idea that looks great on paper and viable; however, the hard part is designing a means by which to measure program outcomes or benchmarks. Evaluating a program throughout the creation and implementation phase is vital to knowing what works, what does not work, and how to improve the program in all areas, including not just on a consumer level, but at the institutional level.

Many times it is easy to develop a leadership program; however, the hard part is measuring its success or lack thereof. There are always opportunities to improve a program, create more efficiency and added value for both the consumer and organization. For example, if you are designing a new leadership program for students, there are many questions that must be answered, such as:

1) What are some potential tools that can be used to measure expected outcomes/benchmarks?
2) What developmental changes are expected in participants as a result of completing the leadership program?
3) How will student proficiency be measured as it relates to the curriculum?
4) How will the leadership curriculum be aligned with other academic disciplines?
5) What are the teaching standards that student participants will be engaged in?

These are just some questions that must be answered when designing a new leadership program for students. There are many tools to measure student success within a leadership program and a combination of these tools can be deployed: portfolios, field exercises, a rubric scoring system, peer and self evaluations, and pre and post assessments. When designing a program of any type it is important to always communicate with an array of stakeholders, departments, and potential participants to design the best possible curriculum and program. The main objective is to have participants reach set goals through a series of exercises and programming that you believe are vital for consumers of that program.

I find it easier to first design the program evaluation outline before developing the entire curriculum. Knowing what you expect from the program—the outcomes you want your end users to come away with once exiting your program and the tools by which you will measure the success of the program—will help guide your research into the resources and curriculum that will best serve your end users and your team. Part of the performance management structure that I used at District of Columbia Public Schools (DCPS) as a means to achieve overall goals, such as designing a viable student leadership program, was to: plan, monitor, develop, rate, and celebrate.

**Plan:** determine the work ahead, set the expectations, and create goals.

**Monitor:** determine the progress you hope to achieve, the obstacles and opportunities that will join you on that journey, and how to measure success and prevent failure.

**Develop:** improve the capacity of the employees and organization to achieve at high levels, introduce new skills, and improve processes and reduce organizational road blocks.

**Rate:** hold everyone involved accountable, determine the success or failure of set goals and performance.

**Celebrate:** recognize success when it occurs, give due credit, and reward efficiency and high performance.

Whatever you choose to design and implement in terms of programming, make sure you plan accordingly and ask all the tough questions. You can never prepare too much for something you believe in and wish to see others succeed at.

## Reaching the Masses: Innovation

Some of the most successful companies in the history of business created their success over adversaries due to an unyielding ability to create innovative products and services. However, for many of these companies, such as Apple, Microsoft, Amazon, Wal-Mart, and McDonalds, they are not always creating something entirely new; usually it is just a tweak of an existing product or service. Take for instance music devices such as CD Players, radio players, eight tracks, and MP3 players. These devices all do the same thing: play music! So what makes the creation of an iPod, which does the same thing as other music devices, more successful than its counterparts? Design, marketing, functionality, and the novelty of creating a new product for consumers are just some of the reasons for the success of the iPod.

We can also look at some of the dynamics of a political campaign for answers. There could be two seemingly similar candidates who support the same issues, but for some reason one is more popular with the public over the other, because of how she looks, her ability to relate and communicate more effectively through numerous modes of media; financial capabilities, experience, energy, and most importantly, her message. The successful campaign was able to match the mood and ideals of voters or a generation at that moment in history.

An obviously great example is the election of Barack Obama as President of the United States. He surely was not the first man of color to run for the Presidency, his ideas were not any different than most of his democratic opponents, nor did he have the same type or amount of experience; however, he was able to tap into a certain mood within the country aching for change. His ability to resonate with voters of all ages, his campaign's ability to raise unlimited cash—primarily from small donors, the candidate's energy level, and his ability to tap into the innovations of social media all helped him overcome the qualms of race, limited national political experience, and the grueling pace of an historic campaign for the highest office in the nation.

I believe there are very telling signs and ideas that we can pull from political campaigns and the business world. There is no guarantee of long-term success, nor of ultimate victory every single time; however, by asking the tough questions, aiming to be different, learning from the failures of others, communicating, and utilizing the amazing capabilities of social media, businesses and political candidates can flourish in a time of unparalleled competition and innovative prowess. Many times it only takes a minor tweak to create real and positive change in the business and public sector. Innovation does not always require starting from scratch and re-inventing the wheel, instead it may just need a new face lift. Take a look around and begin to observe the simple qualms of daily life and discover new and better ways of doing things, then you too can affect real innovative change!

## Living Your Own Story and Discovering Your Purpose

At some point in all of our lives we each evaluate our current situation and where we want to be in the present and the future. We think about the people we want to connect with, the issues that are important to us, and the experiences that will shape our lives. I think about the grind we all eventually find ourselves in every day, that moment when we wake up and hit the snooze button multiple times or the days that seem to go on forever. We are gradually waiting for that day of intense happiness and satisfaction from our current predicaments, that moment in which all the pieces of the puzzle are united and our life has found its true purpose. For many, it comes sooner, rather than later—as for the rest of us, we find ourselves searching for that ultimate meaning on a regular basis in the jobs we do every day, the people we connect with, the societal norms that we find ourselves deviating from, and the special moments in our lives that keep the hope alive that one day our own story will have a perfect ending even if the beginning and the middle of our life story was not all that exciting or easy.

After having a really interesting and compelling conversation with an acquaintance to discuss opportunities in Congress in Washington, DC and politics in general, the conversation quickly turned to the meaning of life and happiness: the moment in which everything converges together to create a perfect equilibrium of success and purpose. There were many important points that I took away from that conversation that I think we all grapple with and intensely thirst for, much like a camel in the desert in search of water. Firstly, we search for happiness in our own lives, including our job, family, social environment, and everyday life. We want to believe in the power of hope and opportunity and that everyone will find his or her ultimate purpose and be free to live without barriers. The idea that every person's life is either a two-hour movie which starts off quite discombobulated but quickly turns into a perfect ending, or a life that is a very long book that takes many turns, twists, lost opportunities, until that final chapter where it all makes sense (I suppose most of us will have the book life).

Secondly, many of us forget that we should take a step back to breathe and enjoy life! We should not allow our careers to define the lives we live. Sure, the careers we choose to take may define pieces of us, but separating the two is vital to understanding the ultimate purpose of each of our lives and treating every experience as a learning opportunity. The individual I met with talked about how he started out wanting to be a doctor, much like his older brother, so he started medical school, but quickly discovered it was not for him. He ended up studying an amazing mix of other programs such as classics, Spanish, economics, and environmental management. It made me think about how as a kid I always begged my parents to let me do something different every day, from acting to business to government. I have always been intrigued by the idea of just learning everything that each of our hearts and minds crave! We should satisfy our cravings for knowledge and purpose through learning. Treat every conversation, job, social experience, success, and failure as a stepping stone to something bigger and greater.

We should never stop questioning and challenging each of our own motives for what we do. Is it for the money? Are we truly happy? If not, what will make us happy? How do we each get there? What is the game plan and ultimate purpose? If we do not allow ourselves to be fully engulfed in the trials and tribulations we face daily, eventually each of our stories will be a success. These stories will be intertwined into the very fabric of life and happiness, creating one for the history books. It is in those times of joy that we truly live. Our senses are fully awakened and our ability to create positive social change is at its highest peak. Since our lives are consistently developing each and every day, spend some time to not just think about life, but live each moment of life as if it is your last! Taking calculated risks will create new opportunities that you may have never imagined, or they may finally open doors to dreams that you have always believed in and knew would come true someday. Savor every experience, every conversation, and every moment—use it as a learning experience to grow and inspire others around you. And with that your own story will become a reality.

## Empowering a Generation: Where Do We Stand?

Even in the toughest of times, we can always find solace in knowing that history tells us those who keep believing and working towards goals greater than one's self will eventually succeed. Generation Y has been brought up in one of the most challenging times in our nation's recent history. The increased prospect of terrorism, economic calamity, joblessness, debt, and an ever changing global economy leaves many wondering exactly what the future will hold for this ever-hopeful generation.

As a member of Generation Y, I too am constantly contemplating what exactly the coming years will look like as America and so many other nations face the unique challenges of today. Our generation is high-tech, connected, hopeful, creative, and under the belief that anything is possible if we just believe. However, as many young people are graduating from college and deciding exactly what their hopes and realities truly look like, many are left puzzled and lost.

Our generation has been rocked the most in terms of unemployment during the 'Great Recession' and the future looks similarly bleak. Companies that generally hire younger workers through job fairs and intensive recruiting have greatly decreased these opportunities due to the flood of qualified older applicants. As our generation depends more and more on parental support, part-time work, and individual endeavors for economic gain and support, what are we to do to become fully independent and successful? Our generation has to rise up to the challenge, as many generations have before us. We must become innovators, thinkers, builders, and entrepreneurs charting our own course in history. As our economy begins to recover, so must we. The times we live in will only become tougher and more diverse in terms of global competitiveness and innovation. And due to this, our generation is uniquely qualified to lead the way.

Discovering who you are, how you can contribute to society as a whole, and planting the seeds of success will be instrumental in each and every person's ability to make a positive difference in the world. We all realize the challenges we face are tough and uncharted, but through those challenges come the opportunity to really make a difference. Believing in one's own innate and learned abilities is important to realizing one's own capacity and talents to not only empower oneself to make real change, but also to empower others. Having hope and faith in a brighter future will go much further in opening new doors to unique quests and aspirations than just living in a constant state of hopelessness. Let us reject the idea of hopelessness and complacency and instead embrace a new conquest to realize our full potential to be positive agents in an ever changing national and global landscape.

## The Invisible Wires of Life

One day while walking to work, I thought about how most people accept the daily grind, the mediocrity, and the hopelessness that life can become, but at the same time they never meant for it to happen, at least not so early in life, and I surely do not want to be in that predicament. As children, our ambitions, hope for life and longevity are endless; there is nothing and no one that can dim that light, only our own individual dabbles into irrelevant and useless side distractions. Sometimes the creative and innovative sparks that eclipses even the darkest moments of our lives and failings as human-beings, loses its energy. However, that is not to say it is gone forever or irreplaceable. The human mind is always changing, we are always learning—for better or worse. There is nothing, except the frailties and decline of human life itself that can negate the power of the human cause.

Our urges to build, design, create, innovate, discover, and shape, are all defining characteristics of our existence and our link to a shared common humanity. The goal of life is always to make it better, either through our own individual means or through the development of some form of shared innovations. We can simply look at such fields as medical research, technology, transportation, etc. The advancements in these fields have categorically changed the way we all live on this earth one way or the other at some point or another, the decisions we each make within our own life maps affect those around us, either because of our inaction to become a part of society and the goal of human life or because of our actions, both positive and negative.

Travis Fine, the mind behind a little known film called, *"The Space Between"*, describes this human connection as being linked by "invisible wires". The concept is based on the idea that even if we may not know the other person or have any relevant relationship, we can still have an effect on that individual and others. The question then becomes how we break free from the shackles of mediocrity and the feeling of being stuck in the quick sand of life itself or the complacency of now. Simply put, in the words of George Washington Carver, *"When you can do the common things of life in an uncommon way, you will command the attention of the world."* Success, happiness, relevancy, and the idea of being a part of something greater than ourselves, are not life qualities that only certain people in certain demographics or socioeconomic backgrounds aspire to. All humans search and grapple for these opportunities to live.

When we as a people realize that living our life goals and making a positive difference in the world is not just about the financial benefits, but also about what we each leave behind and the lives we change, then the difference between mediocrity and excellence will be greatly exposed. Positive thinking, believing in one's own life skills, living life to the fullest, never giving up, and getting the attention of the world by defeating mediocrity and developing an innovative drive, should be the guiding light of our time here on earth. The choice is quite simple: either the individual will fail to take hold of his or her own life success, living in a repetitive state of ordinary being, or he or she will turn the art of ordinary into extraordinary and see life as a means to mold, shape, design, develop, and build, ultimately understanding and embracing the interconnectedness of the human spirit and existence by way of the invisible wires of life.

Viewing life as an opportunity to live, not just for the selfish vices and individualistic gain of oneself, but for the whole of mankind, you learn that there is much more to experience, to gain, to influence, and make better. Everyday there are living examples of individuals who attempt to use their own influence to positively impact the lives of others, such as Bill and Melinda Gates, Oprah, and Lance Armstrong, just to name a few; and then there are those who do not have the notoriety as a high powered celebrity, who are making positive impacts in their communities every day. You do not have to be powerful, wealthy, or well-connected to experience the invisible wires effect, just be you and go where your heart and soul leads you. Live a life that seeks to make the art of common characteristics merely a stepping stone for what is possible.

# 4
# PLANTING A SEED AND CHANGING THE WORLD

*"When you can do the common things of life in an uncommon way,*
*you will command the attention of the world."*
--George Washington Carver

Once you have faith and live everyday to achieve your life's purpose, it is now time to plant the seed of success to ultimately change the world. Every human, no matter how young or old, is capable of positively impacting the society around them. It all starts with an idea and big thinking that will ultimately grow into something greater than one could ever imagine. This section will seek to challenge Generation Y to think not just locally, but globally. How can he or she improve mankind through a spirit of idealism and creativity? That is the goal and this section will answer those probing questions.

A) Mapping your big idea(s).
B) Utilizing others to change the world.
C) Knowing your strengths and weaknesses to create positive change.
D) Creating an aura of positivity for success.

## Planting a Seed and Changing the World

I have come to the full realization that life is one tough journey and it should be taken in nice, short steps setting the stage for the grand finale. Now, that does not mean it will be easy or fast, but to the contrary, there will be many ups and downs, confusion, and upsets; however, failure and learning from that failure will lead to greater success and prosperity in the future. There is such gratitude and strength in believing in yourself and always reminding yourself that you really can do it, whatever that doing is. Giving up or scaling back should never be an option, but shooting for greatness and the top should be a mandate in everyone's life.

It is said that it takes 10,000 hours of work/practice to become an expert or great in life at a particular subject or talent. So if you begin working on something in your elementary school years and truly believe in yourself, by the time you are in your 20s you should be one of the best at it. Think of your life as a garden, one that must be nurtured, pruned, watered, and taken care of. You need a nice mix of sunlight and nutrients to be successful or in normal terms, you need a plan, a vision, and the will power to achieve full success. You must see every day as a step in the right direction—never succumbing to self-doubt or any doubt.

You must believe when no one else dares to believe, fight for success when others are turning their backs, and live out the change and potential you wish to see from yourself and from others. My formula for success is fairly simple: everything you do, believe, think about, work for, and envision for your present and future life, should be the motivation in all that you do. It takes a long time to achieve ultimate success in life, which is defined by the goals you have set and reach that are not only based on success, but happiness. Doing anything that does not make you happy is never right and only leads to wasted time and an unhealthy lifestyle. Think about what makes you happy in life, that provides a comfortable and secure lifestyle for you and do it! Do not be afraid to cross new barriers, to knock on new doors, to dream big, and make known how you plan to change the world!

### The Genetics of a Leadership Mind

Leadership is one of those complex and intriguing issues that is debatable from many different angles. Many people define a great leader as having unique leadership qualities that are in the blood and cannot easily be taught. Yes, you can learn how to run an organization or the right things to say in certain situations, but there is something special about those who have the natural ability to get people on board to fight for an important issue, or to be able to make change happen in a fiery and complex situation, and to come out of that situation unscathed. Genetic leaders are those who have the mind for innovation, forward-thinking insight, and the ability to speak and convey complex issues in a simple, but powerful manner. And in America, we have many of those genetic leaders. One example is Apple founder Steve Jobs, whose natural feel for technology and the ability to integrate those components in our lives in such a fast, unique, and compelling manner, have changed the way we interact with one another.

Also to be considered a genetic leader is former Sec. of State Colin Powell, whose knack for military matters and his ability to lead and instruct in tough, critical situations without getting bogged down in the complexity of the situation, leaves many wondering what is next for the great general. There are many leaders who fit this profile and have all three vital components that make a genetic leader. Forward thinking and an innovative mind is essential for any leader. Innovation is the ability to see something old, something used, in an entirely new light. Those who are innovative think of what is next, rather than what has been done. Innovative leaders see new barriers that need to be broken to make our lives more efficient, safe, entertaining, and unique. In order to be innovative, you must be forward-thinking.

Always seeing a new frontier and possibility for something greater than life itself is the ultimate mission. Many people tend to only see what is in front of them and sometimes even behind them, where as genetic leaders see great things, new doors of opportunity, and aspirations for greatness. In order to make something happen, you must be willing to see past the next day and the next years in order to see something so great and monumental that can change the world for the better. In order to bring those innovative, forward-thinking ideas to the forefront and get people seeing the dream and visions that you hold, you must have the ability to speak and convey complex matters in a unique and powerful manner.

Many people harness great ideas for new products, services, or a strong belief for political change, but yet are unable to write or speak those ideas to others in a way that gets people interested and excited about their cause for action. Genetic leaders have that knack for getting people on board and believing and fighting for the ideals they believe in. With so many mixed and controversial messages out there, true leaders must be able and willing to take a forceful and convincing stand to bring about positive, innovative, and forward-thinking change in the way we as citizens live, act, play, and see the world.

Genetic leaders must be willing to fight for what they believe in and never falter in the face of adversity, but see a challenge as a new beginning to something bigger and greater than them. Genetic leaders must not get used to the way things are or always have been, but to fight for positive change that will bring about growth and innovation to old ideas and old ways of thinking. Nothing great was ever achieved in

America by someone who was weak and did not stand up for their beliefs and fight for what they felt was right and just. The mind of a genetic leader is a mind that is continuously thinking, evolving, and craving for something new, something great, and influential that can change the world for the better. The genetic leader is not afraid to face a challenge or a steel wall, because he or she is able to look beyond that barrier and see a plan, an idea, and a way out, a way to something beyond the imagination of the common human mind.

To be a genetic leader is to not follow the rules set by someone before you, but to always find a way around them in order to make a new beginning and a positive improvement in the way things are done in that respective field. Rules that hamper creativity and idealism are made to be broken by genetic leaders, because they hamper innovation and they hamper improvements to the bureaucratic system that entangles most of the world today in corporate America, in our education system, and most infamously, in Washington, D.C. Being a genetic leader means always looking for something new to bring about a more idealistic and forward-looking change to an old policy, or an old idea. Genetic leaders are always looking to ask questions, to offer new suggestions for positive change, and to open new doors to innovation in the lives of all citizens.

Genetic leaders are not afraid to stand in the spotlight in order to shine light on barriers that need to be broken, on problems that need to be solved, on rules that need to be broken, on issues that need to resolved, and most importantly, to shine light on better ways to do something that has always been done the same way. Genetic leaders do not see the past, sometimes not even the present; they see a whole new world, a whole new way of thinking that cannot be explained, that cannot be seen, that cannot sometimes even be proved to those who do not hold the traits of a genetic leader. We are all born with special abilities, with special ideas, and special goals and visions. Not one human being is made the same way, but we are all uniquely made to defeat certain challenges, to solve certain problems, and to make a positive difference on the Earth for the short period of time we are here.

Genetic leaders, you must not be afraid to stand up to the challenges you face to change the world for the better, but see these great opportunities as the way to something new and something your imprint is made for. Open your eyes, your mind, your heart and soul, to the challenges America and the world face, to use your God-given leadership abilities to crumble walls and open new doors of innovation and opportunity to a people who truly need and desire it. In the words of former

President Woodrow Wilson, *"When you come into the presence of a leader of men, you know that you have come into the presence of fire - that it is best not incautiously to touch that man - that there is something that makes it dangerous to cross him."*

## Imagination is the Foundation of Life!

For centuries, many of the world's greatest leaders, philosophers, entrepreneurs, and thinkers have lived by a simple, yet provocative law: The Law of Attraction. This law is characterized by believing in one's own goals and self; and doing so will fulfill your destiny in life. Many of us wake up daily without a positive attitude and without a path to success. We simply go about our day not really giving much thought to the positive things around us and our own imaginations. Just think back when you were a child, always thinking of new games, ways to beat boredom, and you actually brought those creative ways of thinking to life. Yet as you got older, you simply let the problems of the world push you down and halt your thinking and imagination. You let the negative overtake the positive, and you simply lived day by day without giving any thought to what tomorrow held for you.

However, I have very good news for you; it is never too late to turn back the clock of negativity, sadness, hopelessness, and loss of imagination. Great people, such as Gandhi, Martin Luther King Jr., Einstein, Jesus, Henry Ford, and Winston Churchill, just to name a few, adopted this philosophy of life. As kids, growing up we read about them throughout our classes in amazement. We wondered how these individuals could invent such things, create such hope, and inspire so many people. These great individuals followed their dreams, hopes, and aspirations without regard to the trials and tribulations they would face or the failures they incurred on their way to success. They believed in something, they put one foot out in front of the other, even when they did not have the answer, and they made their imaginations come true. Each and every day we are all capable of doing great things and bringing our hopes and dreams to fruition.

We can go about each and every day complaining, moaning, and blaming everyone else for our problems in life. We can go to work not liking our job, we can stay in a relationship that is not working, or we can bring about positive change in our lives and start anew. Everyone has the power to bring about a new and improved lifestyle, which in the end brings about a better world. What you think and believe is what will come about. Think positive, do positive things, give to others, work daily towards short and long-term goals, and most importantly, never quit imagining. Look around you—your computer, phone, books, desk, etc. These are all created items from the imagination and hands of man. Never forget that you too are capable of great things!

I challenge you to start that business idea you have always dreamed of, to finish the poem you never finished, and most importantly, to stop making excuses. What you have today is enough to bring about the imaginative and powerful change that we are all capable of doing. The story of lottery winners always intrigues me. Lottery winners always seem to be less off financially than most folks, but at the same time they are happy, thoughtful, and have played for years upon years always hoping, dreaming, and knowing that one day, they would win. In addition, when that day comes, we see them on the news and we say to ourselves, "wow, I wish that was me!" Just wishing for something good to happen in our lives is not enough—we must act! You can be and do anything you believe in. That does not mean it is going to happen overnight, but I guarantee you, what you imagine can and will come true through positive thinking and dedication. Your life can start anew today—stop looking at those that have more than you with envy, instead look at those people for inspiration—for the drive to empower your own life to do great things. Remember that your thoughts of hope or failure are, essentially, what you will get. Think and do positive, because that is where greatness of life will show its amazing glory.

### Generation Y: Are We Ready to Take Charge for Positive Change?

We are the future leaders of this world and our decisions today will affect the standards, morals, and policies of this country and world. Either the world will look at us and say "wow, this future generation of leaders and Americans stood for something, they fought for educational reform, helped those who were unfortunate, and they strived to make the world a better place," or they will see a generation that was apathetic to politics, apathetic to positive change and education, and apathetic to making a difference. I know it is hard to imagine how we are supposed to take a stand, how we are supposed to initiate this change and revolution, but simply put, we must act.

We must act in the way of voting, debating, volunteering, recruiting, and taking a stand. In order to act we must educate ourselves on the issues, the candidates, public policy, and how we can make a real difference. Knowledge is the most powerful weapon when it comes to debating and working for change. I believe that we are the next generation to bring about this peaceful revolution of ideas, excitement, involvement, and most importantly, change. To simply not act in this pivotal time would be equivalent to allowing a whole generation to simply erase itself from the history books.

There are so many issues that are at a very important stage of change in our history—education reform, health care reform, social security, the future of our environment, and so forth. We have the opportunity to take charge of these issues and to shape them to fit the needs and wants of our generation. A generation that is idealistic, passionate, creative, and willing to take risks for a better tomorrow. I challenge you to simply not fight for your own survival, but for our nation's survival. No one is promised tomorrow, so we must live everyday as if it is our last. In the words of President John F. Kennedy, *"A revolution is coming - a revolution which will be peaceful if we are wise enough; compassionate if we care enough; successful if we are fortunate enough - but a revolution which is coming whether we will it or not. We can affect its character; we cannot alter its inevitability."*

## A New Type of Entrepreneur

There has been so much focus on the world's financial markets and their instability over the last couple of years. With the stock market shrinking, investments weakening, and consumers not spending, among many of other financial headaches, an open window is forming for a new type of entrepreneur—social entrepreneur. Social entrepreneurs are those who seek to create solutions for the world's social ills, whether it be inadequate education in inner cities, or providing AIDS education to those in Africa, social entrepreneurship is a necessary and exciting way of bringing about positive and real change in the world.

Whereas, business entrepreneurs seek to build products and services that provide great financial incentives for the entrepreneur, social entrepreneurship seeks to build long-lasting solutions for people, so that whole civilizations and groups are able to create and build upon that positive change and influence. Social entrepreneurship can be quite exciting and innovating in a world that craves solutions to so many social and institutional problems. There are many examples of great social entrepreneurial programs, such as the Peace Corps, which have allowed thousands of Americans with so many skills to reach out to impoverished nations, teaching citizens to take hold of their own lives and create economic opportunity for years and decades to come.

There are those in medicine who have created HIV/Aids Information programs—teaching those in Africa and other nations not just how to protect themselves, but the causes of sexually transmitted diseases and how they can pass vital
health lessons on to future generations. Social entrepreneurship aims to empower
people by giving them the knowledge and expertise so that they too can expand
those same goals of independence, entrepreneurship, and idealism for generations to
come. If you are as concerned as I am about the social ills plaguing the world, please
consider using your own skills and creative juices to become a social entrepreneur
and truly change the world.

### Institutional Change is Vital for Social Change

Recently I participated in an exercise meant to show the great divide amongst our social
classes in America. Those classes were lower, middle, and upper, with each class tasked
with purchasing buildings for their new community, such as houses, hospitals, and
schools. However, the twist was that each group did not know immediately which class
they belonged to. The wealthier the social class, the more money they received and the
poorer the social class, the less money they received. I was a "permit employee," so I was
tasked with selling building permits to each class or community. I was told to make it
extremely hard for the lower class to purchase building permits, somewhat hard for the
middle class, and extremely easy for the upper class. Although it was just a simple
experiment that myself and fellow City Year corps members participated in, it really
showed the divide in our social classes, which our nation has been based on since our
existence and the powerful effect that institutions have on shaping and influencing the
success and opportunity, or lack thereof, within social classes.

We always hear our leaders preach how government is supposed to work for the
people, not against them, and even in the Declaration of Independence where it
proclaims that "all men are created equal." However, that is not exactly what has
happened or is happening today. Our nation has clearly lived by a different set of
standards when it comes to reality. Those who live in poor, dilapidated neighborhoods, have a much higher chance of engaging in illegal activity and being caught,
than those who live in upper-class communities. The chance for economic opportunity and success are greater for those who live in communities that are safe, clean,
educated, and modern. However, we should not see that as a means to become angry
at those individuals, as most people do not ask or determine their social class. That is

why we must do all in our power to create a society in which the lack of social justice and equal opportunity is not just a rallying cry for a couple of election days out of the year, but a long-term fight for the rebuilding of a nation and its people.

The failure of one of us is a failure for all of us. An uneducated child in the streets of our nation's capital or a rural family in the hills of Tennessee deserves the same opportunities that those in wealthier communities have been so greatly blessed with. Creating this vital social change is not just about volunteering or donating to a homeless shelter or building a school here and there, it is about changing the fundamental purpose and structure of our institutions here in America. Institutions ranging from our prison system—which needs to focus on rehabilitation, rather than a continuous cycle of incarceration, to our education system—that is too focused on standardized testing, rather than treating each and every child as a human and individual that has his or her own dreams and hopes for life, to our health care system—which is sorely unable to provide affordable basic health care for all Americans, regardless of race or income. The inequities in our health care system are staggering, considering we spend more than any other industrialized nation, but provide health care that ranks in the middle or close to the bottom compared to other wealthy, developed countries.

Our institutions can be better, which does not mean we need a socialist government- controlled society. However, government's task is to work for the people, to ensure fair and equal treatment in all realms of policy, to protect and defend us, and to seek solutions to national epidemics and problems. We can truly do better than the statistics and realities have shown us. We are a better and stronger people than our current and past actions sometimes define us as. In order to bring about the social change our society so greatly needs for long-term survival, we must first look long and hard at our institutions and get rid of what is not working and strengthen those programs and policies that are working. Change can be very hard for many people, but change is vital for the survival of our nation and all of our futures. The moral compass of America and its leaders has been quite lost over the last decade and has contributed to too many issues and problems plaguing us today. How we treat our fellow neighbors is essential to the lives we live today and the lives we hope our children will live down the road. How do we bring about true institutional change, resulting in real social change?

We now understand that institutions are vital in social change, as they provide the mechanisms in which all people are able to move up in social class and economic mobility. The bigger question is how can we cut through the red tape and simplify/reform the bureaucracy in which we live in today? First and foremost educate yourself by learning about issues and institutions that are important to you. If you care about reforming our education system and philosophy of teaching, learn policy in and out, and create your ideal school.

If you want to reform health care, become a health care policy adviser for a senator, so you can directly affect the laws and policies that determine the future of health care policy. Educating yourself empowers your own thinking and helps to create a foundation of solutions and ideals that will last a lifetime and give you a true means to create lasting social change. The battle will not be easy, nor will it always be fun, but remember that your fight and your struggle today for social justice and institutional change will create a new beacon of hope and idealism for the next generation.

## What Will You Shape?

One of my favorite books, *The Alchemist*, truly inspired me to see the world as a means to success and positive change, not so much the end, but a new beginning. The notion that we all have a personal legend or a purpose is both challenging and uplifting. As we go about our daily lives, the people we meet, the paths we cross, and the challenges we face are all connected to bringing us closer to our life's mission. The challenge for all of us is to jump in somewhat blindfolded and put our trust in our faith and beliefs to never lead us astray, but to bring us ever closer to our purpose in this life. The ability within all of us to shape the world in our own liking is quite amazing. The fact that we can create, write, mold, inspire, and drive the present as well as the future is a tool that we should not take for granted.

A society built on sound moral principles and innovative drive is not just a hope of radicals or fanatics, but a hope of all people who see a world that is free, open, and strong in its belief that when people come together, united for a common purpose, they can truly shape the world for the better. When Memorial Day approaches every year, it is a time to remember those who gave the ultimate sacrifice so that we can continue to take up and pass on the mantle of life, liberty, and the pursuit of happiness. Through our service to others in all facets of life, we can inspire a generation, lift up a hopeless people, and bring about a new zest for life and happiness to the world. America has always been a beacon of hope and justice to millions across the world, and there is no reason why we should turn our back on the world in times of strife and struggle; instead we must let our most challenging times be a new model for success, determination, and perseverance.

The world will forever be shaped by the will and hands of mankind. However, the question that always remains is, what exactly will this world look like? How will we treat the least of us? How will we solve some of the most complex and challenging social and political ills? Our hands and minds are the key to a great and prosperous future or one that fails to adhere to our core American values of liberty and freedom. We shall create a future that brings about a hopeful and idealistic generation that is ready to rise up to the challenges of today, tomorrow, and forever in order to create, mold, build, and inspire a more just and free society. What is your purpose? What is your call to greatness and the legacy that you will leave? We all have one, but it is up to you to figure it out and to follow that path of greatness so you too can shape the world for the better.

## Cause the Effect: The Revolution of Ideas

We have all heard the term "cause and effect" which is the idea that one event is directly related to the outcome of another. I came across one of America's top political consulting firms online, GMMB, and their slogan "cause the effect" really hit me and made me think how all of us have the power to affect positive change. The choices we make in our lives—from college decisions to career choices to family decisions—all have an impact on the social fabric of our nation and our world. Every decision we make causes something else to occur, either positive or negative. I would hope that we all aim to create positive outcomes in the decisions we make.

Most importantly, when I look at education in this country and the negative impact we are leaving on our children, I am deeply troubled. Our ability to educate and empower a new generation of thinkers, builders, artists, and socially aware citizens is of utmost importance. Throughout this country and world, there are many children who are being shortchanged in their educational opportunities, and it is truly a travesty. We have a noble obligation to see to it that every child has at least an opportunity to live out whatever dream he or she has for their life and future. And by doing so, not only are we ensuring a better society based on strong social values, but also an idea that as citizens of this Earth we shall leave it better off than we found it.

We are all capable of doing amazing things and all of us have talents and creative juices that run through our blood and minds every single day; however, it is our responsibility to make those ideals and hopes a reality. We have had many amazing people in our lifetime that have taken up causes of freedom, prosperity, the environment, technology, medicine, and so much more—people such as Mother Theresa, Bill Gates, Martin Luther King Jr., and Nelson Mandela just to name a few. I challenge you to determine how you can cause the effect, how you can make a positive difference in the world around you, and leave this planet just a little bit better off for future generations.

## Be Different: Power to the People

As kids we were always told that being different was not ok, that it was not the norm or the cool thing to do. Somehow we allowed society to dictate the status quo and what was not possible, instead of what could be possible. And with that came the belief that our ideals and abilities were not inextricably linked to one another or the Earth that we inherited; however, this belief should no longer stand. The people of all nations, beliefs, colors, and creeds have the most solemn promise to one another: that we stand together for a better generation and society than we inherited. The social causes of one nation shall not be only theirs to bare, but of all socially conscious members of society, from people, businesses, non-profit organizations, governments, and the like, to stand up for one another for a brighter future.

The idea of believing in something greater than ourselves is still relevant today, which allows us to be a part of the solution and not just the problem. There are so many social causes that demand our utmost attention and evaluation: HIV/Aids, genocide, poverty, infectious diseases that ravish developing nations, education, clean water, innovative solutions to climate change, health care, war, economic development, and so much more. Sometimes we become so beholden to what "has" been done, instead of what "should" and "can" be done. We forget about our moral and ethical obligations to one another to build a more prosperous, healthier, and productive Earth. Through the empowerment of others we can change the status quo, give hope to the hopeless, and a voice to the speechless. Some ways that you can do this is by supporting organizations and political candidates that fight for social causes you believe in, speaking out when a social injustice is occurring by writing to a local newspaper, or even starting your own campaign to bring about social change to an issue that matters deeply to you.

Being different is a good thing. Changing how systems work to be more efficient for the greater good, reaching the masses to create real social change, and educating a society on the social challenges of our time are all within the realm of possibility. Being different is the norm, not the exception. What do you believe? How can you be different?

## Ideas Really Do Change the World: What Have You Thought About Lately?

There are solutions to most complex problems that we face in the world today. Problems as grave as poverty, climate change, HIV/AIDS, health care reform, war, the destruction of our forests, and so forth. If you really think about it, there has always been a solution to most problems that we face today, even if the technology or science or will is not always there, the idea is. When you look at the steady advancements of flight that started with the Wright brothers, known for building the first successful plane, there were many people before them that envisioned flying and created a means to do so. Flight innovators viewed the skies as a new means of travel and exploration. When the Wright brothers' first flight took off, you can only imagine their hope that one day future inventors would develop a means to travel to the heavens above. Now look how far we have come in terms of air and space travel.

We know that there can be a cure for HIV, and as science advances, the hard work placed into making this goal a reality will pay off. We also see a stark reality detachment by many who deny that greenhouse gases are destroying our ozone layer. Simply by denying that humans have not played a major role in increasing pollution and greenhouse gases leading to the warming of the Earth, i.e. climate change, is by far the most ignorant and unintelligent way to handle a problem that exists and gravely impacts our Earth as we know it today. The first step to solving a problem is to admit it exists. The second step is to then map out the problem and determine its cause(s). Thirdly, once the cause of the problem has been determined it is time to research solutions. These solutions should not automatically be thrown out at face value. Numerous sources and ideas must be engaged and thought through to create the best solutions to complex issues.

For instance, let us look at poverty. Clearly people are starving, jobless, and homeless for many reasons ranging from a lack of economic means or ability, physical and/or mental handicaps, and the inability to find employment over a long period of time, debt, and so forth. These are some causes of poverty, now what would be some solutions? Job training programs could be improved and expanded for those seeking work and those who are able to work; increased economic incentives for people to attend college or trade school; help those in debt seek financial counseling and planning; and increased mental health counseling for those who are able to work, but are not yet mentally or physically stable to do so, just to name a few. Once again the idea is to freely come up with solutions to solve the problems we face through brainstorming.

Everyone has an idea, regardless if they speak out or not. Once people come together and put their minds in the same bucket, we can truly create real solutions for important problems facing our country and globe. If you think you have the next golden idea or solution for a complex or even simple problem, do not be afraid to believe in yourself and your own abilities to make real positive change happen in the world. Just think about some of the most successful people in the world today and those that have passed on: Albert Einstein, Bill Gates, Warren Buffett, Thomas Edison, Jesus, Mother Teresa, Nelson Mandela, and on and on! In the words of Nelson Mandela, he was simply an ordinary man doing extraordinary things. When I think of someone believing in him or herself, I think about the mother or father who works every day, maybe two or three jobs, so their child can live a better life, so that they can dream and make their greatest ideas a reality. Or the entrepreneur who has maybe failed once, twice, ten, maybe twenty times on a business idea, but fails to quit, because he or she believes in what is possible and their own abilities to create real innovation. Lastly, I think of those who deal with war, destruction, and outright poverty who fight for freedom and justice every single day against unjust governments that use tanks and guns as a means of control instead of opportunity and liberty to open new doors for their people.

We face so many challenges in the 21$^{st}$ Century; however, I know that those who dare to dream and believe in the power of ideas, hope, and perseverance will help this society overcome the many failures of our past and the challenges and triumphs of the future. I challenge you not to fear what the future holds, but to tackle it head on with the same energy, resilience, and curiosity of those before us that charted a path of opportunity in so many fields such as medicine, technology, political and economic thought, education, the environment, and so forth. Do not allow yourself to become complacent with mediocrity, but use your zest for life and discovery as a means and inspiration to create your own legacy that will leave this world in a better place.

## The Dream is Just Beginning

We live in such a polarized world today where our own quest for survival comes into direct conflict with our urge for peace and prosperity. Our own hopes for our fellow man become entangled with our own selfish vices. The thirst for inner peace and tranquility clashes with the materialistic society in which we are all born into, where happiness is defined by what we have more than what we give. Our souls know the end of selfishness, murder, greed, lust, envy, and war, but our minds tell us otherwise. We tend to fight fire with fire, we see the need to constantly attack or defend, instead we should be gaining a better understanding of those we chastise and judge, bringing people together, and charting a new path to a more stable and hopeful society.

There is a belief that human nature is unable to exist without war and destruction, that even as we look at the blood of history, we fail to see that the light of tranquility has eventually always overcame the darkness. Even in the midst of struggle, death, and hopelessness, there is always a more just and righteous path. We are all far from perfect as our own lives and paths are littered with the transgressions of our founders and many of us have yet to chart a new course. However, I reject the notion that our past should be the definitive guide for our future.

Shall we forget the past and never turn back? Absolutely not—for the past holds the key to freedom and triumph over evil. We see that our past, regardless of race, creed, or gender, is just as inextricably linked today as it was then. The fight for opportunity, peace, justice, and freedom is a continuous struggle that takes new forms as time ticks silently in the background. The questions that remain then are quite simple: Where shall you stand? Where will your voice be heard? Will it be heard on the side that denounces love and humanity? Or will it sound the echoes of those who stood for social progress and opportunity?

Martin Luther King Jr. once said, *"It may well be that the greatest tragedy of this period of social transition is not the glaring noisiness of the so-called bad people, but the appalling silence of the so-called good people."* We should not deny that there will be opposing sides and ideals, with many that see social progress as a threat to freedom and liberty on one side of the spectrum and on the other, many who see social progress as a means to empower and liberate a generation of people. Then the question becomes, where do we go from there?

Another quote by Martin Luther King Jr. frames our calling quite elegantly, *"We must rapidly begin the shift from a "thing-oriented" society to a "person-oriented" society. When machines and computers, profit motives and property rights are considered more important than people, the giant triplets of racism, materialism, and militarism are incapable of being conquered."* And from this end, we cease to exist as a human-race. When we allow war, hate, worldly possessions, self-gain, and selfishness to conquer our global psyche, we forget our need to care for one another and that the death of one human is the death of many.

We all lose something when human life is lost—we lose a friend, a neighbor, a family member, a stranger, and a piece of life itself within us. But, to someone, somewhere that loss was somebody. Understanding the importance of humanity or the point of human existence is to believe in a higher calling for each of us and acknowledging we all have a special gift that is directly related to our presence on this Earth. If we can accept that idea, then we can move beyond the simple and finite pleasures of this world and move to the human consequences of our actions and positions.

Treating life as a ladder that must be climbed at the expense of the one below us is the definition of selfish ambition—that by destroying another or judging another even as we ask not to be judged ourselves we lose sight of our own need for positive human interaction. When we come to understand that we truly are all made equally, that our lives are truly interconnected, that life itself has a meaning greater than any law, product, or personal endeavor—we will all come to realize that the progression of a positive human race hinges on this ideal as well on the understanding that we are simply a microcosm of a much bigger plan.

We must stop pitting one versus the other in search of the most destructive means possible to create our own individual and selfish legacy. 10,000 years from now, if we continue on a path of destruction, we will be known by no human, dead or alive. If there truly is a higher purpose for each of us, as I believe, then the most important principle that we can all do is to love one another. Through love, true humanity shines—the ability to sympathize with our fellow man and woman brings about a rejuvenation of the soul. Let us remember the principles on which humanity itself best thrives from: hope, love, sympathy, and social progress. Through the empowerment of others to become self-sustaining partners in our quest to improve the social mobility of all, society will once again realize the dream of Dr. Martin Luther King Jr.

## Utilizing Social Media and Solution Based Communication
## to Improve Government Access

Social media has provided a new opportunity for small and large businesses alike to reach out to new customers, to create smart marketing campaigns, and most importantly, to create a new solution based communication structure that allows not just a few and privileged to participate in, but a much wider and more diverse audience. Twitter and Facebook have both been able to tap into this market by connecting businesses, products, and end users together through social media networking. Companies are able to solicit an immediate response from end users while simultaneously developing products and services around that communication.

For example, Vitamin Water created an online campaign that allowed Facebook users to name the company's new beverage product and through online campaigning, people were able to successfully lobby Saturday Night Live to bring famed actress Betty White as a host. What is even more intriguing is that the end users themselves actually become the product creators, testers, and buyers. Consumers of social media have been broadly utilized to spread information about new products and services ranging from new technology launches to political campaigns.

Social media has truly paved the way for innovation that not only starts with the consumer, but ultimately ends with the consumer. This process, if used correctly, can reduce the need for companies to consistently go back to the drawing board to fix problems after the fact. This is especially seen during beta testing for new websites, software, and online products. As businesses have been quick to embrace social media, so to should government at all levels to improve community outreach, promote new initiatives, educate citizens on new laws and ordinances, and lastly, to provide instant announcements and feedback. This would eventually create a solution based communication network.

Government by its own nature should be a tool for the people, by the people. Government agencies, from health to the environment, should consistently reach out to community members to gauge their ideas, opinions, and needs when developing policy. Through the use of social media, government agencies would be able to reach out to community members more efficiently and cost-effectively. Many federal agencies under President Obama have done just that, ranging from the U.S. State Department to FEMA. However, this should not just be a federal government initiative, but also local and state. My local government in Arlington, Virginia actively connected with citizens via Twitter and Facebook to make important announcements during the H1N1 pandemic and also during the winter snowstorms.

Social media is also very useful for government agencies to promote new initiatives and to educate citizens about new laws and ordinances. With approximately 90% of Americans using the Internet[1], access is less of a problem than in years past. Public libraries and the increase of high speed internet have all been very useful in increasing internet access for low income and rural Americans. Many instances when new programs are created or laws are passed; word of mouth and newspapers are utilized as the main source of information. Government agencies should now rely more on social media to do so. It is less expensive and more accessible to individuals to learn more about what their government is or is not doing. Agencies can utilize online video, blogs, and an array of social media tools to educate and promote new programs.

Lastly, social media allows for instant communication and feedback creating a solution based communication network. Social media allows government agencies and citizens to work together throughout the process of creating, promoting, marketing, and implementing new policies and initiatives. Just like many private companies and non-profit organizations, government agencies can make the tedious process of legislating and executing policy more people friendly, open, communicative, and ultimately more successful. Leaders on both sides of the political spectrum must become more in tune with the needs of citizens and the positive impact social media can have on improving the relationship between government leaders and the citizenry. Using social media to announce road closures, new regulations, important announcements, streamlining documents and policies online, and opening a new era in digital communication will be integral for all levels of government to become of age in the new social media environment.

## The Power of Ordinary People to Change the World

What is good in the world? What can we improve? How can we bring about positive sustainable social change, innovation, entrepreneurship, and creativity? How can we solve social ills? The 21st Century challenges all of us to be active participants in making the necessary changes to ensure a stable, growing, efficient, and innovative

---

[1] http://www.internetworldstats.com/stats14.htm#north

society. Learning from others and building new bridges of opportunity for millions of disadvantaged people is vital to the success of a new generation. We must engage, educate, and act in order to see real positive change that can be replicated from community to community. The challenges we face in a global society are evolving constantly and require innovative solutions that bring people and ideas together for the common good.

When great, creative, and idealistic minds are brought together, the possibilities are endless. We all must realize that we can do more together than apart. Even with our differences, we must recognize the complexity of the many social and political ills we face, not just at home, but abroad. Along with this acknowledgment is the understanding of the interconnectedness we as human beings all share, that no matter the distance, barriers, or cultures, we are all citizens of the Earth. We know that we must do more to create and promote new means of clean energy, to spread the wealth of education and knowledge, to invent new medicines and cures, to fund and develop new technologies, to utilize the power of social media to bring people together for the common good, to bring ideas together, and ultimately to empower ordinary people to do extraordinary things. We live in a society that expects quick solutions and results; therefore, it is vital that we understand the full implications of our actions, words, and their overall impact on society as a whole. Once we realize that ideas can change the world, we must then unite to create a more just, open, and free society that spans the globe.

The amazing talent of Generation Y must be realized and tapped into. This generation values a diverse and open society that believes in the faith of ideas and the power of humanity. Once we believe that humanity itself hinges on the hopes and actions of future generations, we can then open our minds and our doors to a new philosophy that understands the power of positive social change. Too often we focus on what is bad and what is wrong and we choose not to act, nor to change it. However, the few that see hope out of fear, ideas out of dreams, and creativity out of destruction are those who change the world. Those individuals are the ones that open new doors and light the path for generations to come. We can do more good together than apart. The ability we all have to see the light at the end of the tunnel, even when there is darkness, will propel us into a future that is brighter and more prosperous then we could have ever imagined. Let us renew our commitment to the power of humanity and to the spirit of social change that is not based on taking away from or tearing down another, but that is rooted in the ideal that all people can be a part of the solution, that all people are capable, that all people are valued and that all people can make a positive difference in the life of another.

## The Power of Thoughts

Thoughts are powerful as they shape our purchasing decisions, political votes, religious affiliations, and our own ideals—ultimately our view of the world. Thoughts have many sources—the media, friends, family, teachers, religious leaders, our own life experiences and so forth. The power of the mind is quite a unique and awe inspiring aspect of being human. It is what shapes our daily interactions with others and how we perceive the world around us. It is vitally important for each of us to monitor what shapes our thoughts and ideals. The messages we take in are quickly part of our daily output. Positive thinking, personal influences and outside environments all play a role in shaping who we are today and in the future.

How we refresh our minds to tend to the daily challenges we face can determine the forces of nature we are a part of changing and influencing. We all have the ability to positively change the world, to love those we do not know, to fight for the plight of those who have not, and to believe in a positive force greater than ourselves. Let not your thoughts be shaped by the negative forces of the world, but instead look towards positive energy and the power of our shared humanity on this earth. Our time is short here, so let us not waste a minute spreading fear and hate; instead let us promote what is good, peaceful, and that which creates positive social change in a world that so dearly needs it.

## Ordinary People and the Power of Extraordinary Actions

"Ordinary People" is a title of a great John Legend song and for me a declaration of who we all are and what we are all capable of being. At the end of the day, no matter how much money we have, the clothes we wear, the jobs and titles we attain, we are all just ordinary people. We all deal with human problems, emotions, controversies, pains, joys and opportunities. Even in our most conflicting moments our humanistic virtues encased in an ever binding thought process show themselves. We all feel the daily pressures of life, the consequences of bad and good decisions, and we all hold idealistic hopes and dreams for younger generations. Case in point, Bill Gates, one of the richest individuals in the world, has everything money can buy and a philanthropic legacy that will surely outlive his most seasoned corporate accomplishments. He has dedicated the rest of his life to ridding the world of curable diseases, promoting education reform and development throughout the world and promoting energy innovation, among a host of other projects.

He sees a world filled with ordinary people. And within this world the success of our generation depends not merely on wealth, but action, not merely of a few good men, but through the empowerment of millions of ordinary people doing extraordinary things. There are many people like Bill Gates throughout the world, rich and poor, famous in terms of media standards, and many who are just local social change agents without worldwide fame or a global platform. Nonetheless, these great people, these ordinary people, are compelled to act in the face of unyielding adversity and obstacles. Where many see an infinite and hopeless struggle to create lasting and sustainable social change, these ordinary people see an opportunity to give hope and prosperity to the down trodden and lost. They see light, where others see darkness, plague, and hopelessness. The question that always remains and is constantly asked is what empowers these ordinary people? I am not sure if there is one right answer. I can only imagine that each ordinary person who dedicates his or her life to extraordinary deeds is inspired by many things such as the challenge, the stories, the people, the opportunity, the gift, the hope, and the promise that a tree planted is a life anew.

The life experiences of each person on this earth are a gift within itself. We all have much to learn, much insight and wisdom to bequeath to future generations. However, we should not merely latch on to this knowledge, but we must share it, build it, design it, and utilize it today to make a real lasting social change through reforming education, empowering young people, creating new technologies, discovering new medicines for debilitating diseases, helping one another, and most importantly, living a life that is not only about us, but about all of humanity. Let our daily decisions, thoughts, and actions be positively impactful on society as a whole. Even with all of our ordinary human flaws, there is a greatness that resides in each of us waiting to be tapped, waiting to be fulfilled, and waiting to be shared with the rest of the world.

# 5
# FINDING YOURSELF,
# BY GIVING OF YOURSELF

*"The value of a man resides in what he gives and*
*not in what he is capable of receiving."*
--Albert Einstein

An ancient proverb from the Holy Bible states "it is better to give than to receive." How do we put this into action in today's society? Living with a virtuous spirit, a heart of warmth and giving, and a mind that is always thinking of improving the lives of others is a start to living a fulfilling and successful life. This section will promote the ideas of social change and giving to help those who have the least to recognize their purpose on this earth.

A) Creating your own movement through service.
B) Social change.
C) Sharing your talents with others.
D) Lifting others up to success.

## Giving is Always Better Than Receiving

Instead of soaking gracefully in the sun or visiting some far away island on an enchanted cruise, I, along with 17 other University of Tampa students spent our Spring Break in 2007 with Habitat for Humanity in Meridian, Mississippi helping bring back a sense of home and normality for families affected by Hurricane Katrina. It was truly an amazing experience that will last with me for a lifetime. One of the families had lost everything due to Hurricane Katrina and was only able to salvage family photos. Another recipient was an older lady who was legally blind and was in need of a new home. The best experience of it all was getting the chance to meet the families who would be staying in these homes and the smiles of joy and appreciation in their hearts.

Community service is an extension of one's heart and soul. It is what makes us who we are as a people—giving, caring, loving, energetic, and imaginative. Those who give and volunteer his or her time, money, skills, or kind words, can only describe the art of helping someone else who is less fortunate. Throughout my life, I have been at the receiving end of giving. As a child growing up in a large, low to middle income family, there were many times when local church folks would bring over food, help with the bills, and come over to our home to spend time with my family. Therefore, I see volunteering as giving back to those who gave to me and those who need the love and care that only humans can provide.

A very important philosophical meaning that showed itself to me while on the trip and continues to do so now is the amazing fact that as humans, we are all so capable of doing great things. Just thinking that with our hands we were capable of building a home—one of the most sacred places for an individual or a family—was a great feeling. Everyday around the world men and women are doing what we did—making lives better, improving living conditions, and so much more with their God-given abilities. It does not take a genius to learn new things in life, even if we have no prior experience. All it takes is the use of our God-given senses and the ability to learn from our mistakes. Life is such a precious gift and I really love the challenge of what it entails. It causes us to think and imagine greater and better opportunities that are not always visible in the present or even in the near future. Nevertheless, there is always a sense of mission and purpose in all of us that we must recognize and hold on to throughout our lives.

Life is so much more about giving than receiving, because what you give will always come back to you so much more abundantly. I truly look forward to what the future holds, not only for myself, but my fellow peers that I hope I touched and enlightened one way or another, as well as for the families we helped and inspired. I praise those who continuously give of themselves in the quest to make the world a better place, because our lives can only exceed the depth of our imagination, so dream big!

## The Spirit of National Service

*"My passionate sense of social justice and social responsibility has always contrasted oddly with my pronounced lack of need for direct contact with other human beings and human communities."*
—Albert Einstein

As these tough economic times create turmoil for many Americans, there is still hope for a better tomorrow. The vision of Americans, young and old, of all races, beliefs, and generations working hand in hand to build a better America from the bottom up, is a vision whose time has come. The belief that we can single-handily alter the course of our nation, no matter how small we believe our acts of social justice are, is upon us. We are all capable of achieving great and inspiring moments through the spirit of service. This spirit of generosity and hope shines brightly today through the single parent who works alongside volunteers with the services of Habitat for Humanity to build their new home after Hurricane Katrina destroyed all of their possessions and memories of life or the child who now has that "Big Brother" or "Big Sister" they have always dreamed of through the Boys and Girls Club. There is a new spirit in America of service, community, and social justice.

Many people believe the only way they can serve their country is through military service. Serving our country through the selfless act of voluntary enlistment in our armed forces is the noblest and most extraordinary of all human sacrifices and humility. However, there are many other means of service right here in our home-land. Organizations such as City Year that are committed to reforming our public school system through the idea that our children are the most important aspect in that process and must be nurtured, mentored, and fought for. You can visit *http://www.americorps.org* and find out which program is right for you, from rebuilding homes in New Orleans, to teaching children in America's inner cities, or beautifying parks and community centers, there is something for everyone.

If you believe in social justice, if you believe in a better America that fights for all people, and if you believe in your own power to bring about positive change, I challenge you to give of yourself in order to inspire a new generation of Americans to fight for a new cause of freedom and prosperity. We are responsible for the future prospects of America and where we will be five or ten years down the road. For those who are soon to be graduates from either high school or college, do not fear the prospect of giving up a year of your life and your talents to serve others. I promise you, the feelings and experiences you gain through the service of others are the most gratifying any one person can feel. Graduate school, law school, medical school, and every other educational opportunity will still be available for you once you are done with your service and also greatly enhanced through scholarship programs and the real world experiences you gain through your service.

We are in a very momentous time in our nation's history and for the first time in a long time, young people are on the forefront of that change and ability to actively build our future today. Take up the challenge and help change America and the world.

### Making the World a Better Place

We have all been told at some point in our lives that we are each capable of changing the world, making it a better place through helping others, and truly realizing our inner potential to inspire and uplift a generation of people. It sounds very cliché, which is probably why most people do not aim to change the world nor change anything for that matter. It is much easier to complain and live with the status quo than to actually get up from a comfortable desk and aim to make a difference. Most importantly, the broadness of such a goal to change the world is a pretty tough proposition. If changing the world is too daunting of a task for you target a more specific issue—to change education, to improve the environment, to inspire young people, etc. The more people are able to connect with a goal and believe in it, the more likely they are to join in the cause.

People are ready to respond—no matter their age, race, or economic background— if they are provided with specific parameters, needs, tools, and ideas to do so. When our economy is faltering, the idea of people coming together and fighting for one another is one dynamic that has always fascinated me and it is a truly amazing objective. The feeling you get from helping one another is one of a kind and cannot be replicated by any other action. Instead of judging others who are not like you, why not stand with them and help them to become who they dream to be?

Volunteering once a week or bi-weekly at a soup kitchen, tutoring kids at a local elementary school, working with Habitat for Humanity, traveling the world helping to build schools or improving health care are all attainable goals that can be reached by one individual or a group of people. You will be inspired and motivated to do more, to fight for more people and in the end you will become a better person because of your own selfless actions. Giving of oneself in the spirit of another is a truly captivating gift and when put into action, real dreams come true in the quest to make the life of another better and ultimately, the world will become better too.

Find a way to make a difference: http://www.idealist.org/
Renew America Together: http://www.usaservice.org/content/home/
AmeriCorps: http://www.americorps.org/

## Finding Your Purpose, By Giving of Yourself

In church one morning I heard a really hopeful message from my pastor that was truly a point of motivation and inspiration for me. I am sure if any of you have read the Bible or your own religious book of scripture even once or heard anything about Jesus, the idea and power of sacrifice and truly submitting one's self to a higher calling, is of utmost prudence. For some reason this idea really stuck to me that morning and I could not stop thinking about it. For many Christians, the Season of Lent is a time to give up something in preparation for Easter and the death and resurrection of Jesus Christ. Instead of simply giving up something, why not choose to do something? It is very important that we recognize the many bad habits we should be working to give up every single day, but there are those habits in which many of us should be choosing to follow and accomplish every day, mainly the act of service and giving to those who are in need.

I think many times we forget about the trials and tribulations occurring to those who cannot lift themselves up, who have no hope or promise, or reason to live. This must be the calling for many of us in order to rise to that challenge and give of ourselves in hope that those who are impoverished, and who live without shelter or education, will gain a new life through our service to them and for them. In times of economic strife and hardship, it is easy to be fully concerned with our own vices, as we should partially, but let us not forget how we can truly impact the world. I applaud those who take up such admirable professions such as nursing, medicine, counseling, teaching, non-profit and faith-based community engagement, national and international service organizations, and so forth. These people are truly the back bone of our civilization and help to provide hope and promise to millions of people worldwide. It is through them that we can still believe that the world is a better place than many of us are led to believe.

For those who are finishing up high school and college or even those who are older, if you feel the need to make a difference, I ask you to challenge yourself, to truly think anew about how you can really change the world. Will you take a year off before graduate school and visit a far away land to teach a young child English or help to build a clean water supply system for an impoverished people? Will you join a national non-profit and work with low-income families so that they too can see the promise of America and what she has to offer to those who believe in sustainable social change? Life is young, therefore every second of your life has a purpose and it is up to you to fulfill your true calling, whatever that may be. Take some time to evaluate who you are, who you want to become, your purpose and how you can be a truly positive and monumental impact in the lives of others in need. I promise that through this service and sacrifice you will come to know yourself more than you ever have before.

## The Emergence of the Web for Social Change

Technology has always been useful in merging communities from different cultures and parts of the world. Technology today is becoming even more useful and prevalent in its ability to unite people and ideas to bring about real social change. A perfect example is President Obama's pioneering use of the web during his campaign for the presidency with the creation of his online social networking community called MyBarackObama or MyBO. MyBO allowed for ordinary citizens to connect with voters all across the country using online phone banking to promote his candidacy. MyBO also allowed members to organize house parties and community canvassing events, to efficiently raise funds in small amounts, and to dispel rumors and actively convey his message of change.

Never before had a candidate, locally or nationally, harnessed the power of the web in such a shock and awe manner that resulted in millions of users, millions of dollars, and thousands of citizens organizing events leading to victory! The World Wide Web is consistently reinventing itself with the likes of Twitter, Facebook, and web entrepreneurs, but it also creates an opportunity for ordinary people to change the world. A family in a small town in need of funds to help their child and his or her cancer treatment can recruit thousands of activists to help raise the money, or a young teenager who has an amazing idea to create a new technology can find hundreds of others who hold similar views and can help spawn a new empire.

If used in a positive manner with an entrepreneurial spirit, the web can be an amazing force for social change and social entrepreneurship. We can bring together people of all ideals, hopes, passions, and needs to revolutionize the way our society helps one another. Through the creation of web sites and use of already established social networking platforms, people can unite their own individual passions with others on a quest to create new industries, new ventures, new technologies and services, and eventually empower a new economy based on self-sufficiency, independence, and social entrepreneurship. When we generally think of business and entrepreneurs, we think of big loans, big buildings, and business suits. However, this stereotype is changing as a new era of young, intelligent, and idealistic entrepreneurs come forth without dreams of big money and fancy cars, but with the intent to actually make a real difference in the world, bringing communities and people together for the betterment of man-kind.

The work of Mark Zuckerberg, the creator of Facebook, is one in which we can point to as a model for a new era in web creation aimed at social change. He has turned down numerous billion dollar offers to sell Facebook, believing that his cause to unite people through social networking is more important than creating something that is fleeting. Mark believes that his work can have a long-lasting effect on his quest to bring people together, making networking and information sharing seamless and easy, and in the end creating more interactive ventures through Facebook itself. The use of Facebook during the Egyptian uprisings proved that social platforms can bring about real change in closed societies. The power of an idea can stretch very far with the emergence of a new web culture that values information, networking, and the power of many voices. As you go about your day, think about how you can positively impact the world and how, through the use of the web, you can unite people with similar interests, hopes, and dreams to make their visions and yours for social change a reality.

## Generation Y: A New Era of Progressive Social Change

Generation Y or the Millennial Generation, those born between 1982 and 2000 totaling more than 80 million young people have truly created a new era of social change and civic engagement. Generation Y has been shaped by war, terrorism, recessions, and a constant flow of information and technology. Those within the millennial generation or Generation Y, overwhelmingly support progressive political candidates and issues, ranging from gay marriage to stem cell research to national service. As a member of this generation myself, we seek the approval of others, thrive on independence and culture, and aim to make a difference in the world in all that we do.

According to a USA Today article, generation y voted overwhelmingly for President Obama by a margin of 2 to 1. Our generation is known for its creativity, love of technology, information, and idealistic tendencies. Many of our parents tend to wonder exactly what we are doing with our lives, especially when we spend so much time "finding ourselves" through service, entrepreneurial ventures, parties, and trips. Our generation parties just as hard as it works as we seek to balance a stressful life with amazing friends, activities, and interactive social experiences to create a well rounded life.

Social networking sites such as Facebook have allowed us to freely express ourselves and our lives on a 24/7 basis, keeping friends studying overseas just as close as friends in the dorm room next door updated on what our daily activities are, from simply cooking some pizza for a Friday night movie or watching our favorite show to constantly updating our Facebook statuses to reflect personal moods and every day happenings. Our generation, more than any other, has been in the center of a new progressive society, poised to make an impact at a young age and driven by the need to stay relevant and empowered.

As time goes on, so will our influence grow and the hope of tomorrow will rest in our hands. Shall we take the challenge and create a new society that embraces inclusion, idealism, volunteerism, and service? Or will we sputter out and become more hesitant to social change and be defined by a need for too much information resulting in a collapse of our social norms and structure? Only time will tell, but my hope is that we will embrace a culture that embodies a fresh hope for tomorrow, a thrill to serve others in need, and tenacity that creates rather than destroys.

### The Role of Government in the 21st Century

Over the last two years and even before then, there has been a renewed debate on the role of government. There tends to be two over arching thoughts on this issue. One argument states that government is ultimately inept and unable to truly make a positive and sustainable difference in the lives of ordinary Americans and another argument that believes government, if utilized correctly, can do well and protect ordinary Americans from the abuses and excesses of privatization and capitalism. I tend to believe there is room for both of these ideological thoughts to ensure that ordinary Americans are protected and given equal opportunity under the law and that government promotes innovation and creativity within private industries without smothering the ideas and measured risk taking of entrepreneurs.

History has shown us the trials and tribulations of both extremes, nation's such as Russia, formerly known as the Soviet Union, crumbling under the heavy hand of communist rule and even our own recent "Great Recession" where corporate excess and limited government regulation enforcement almost brought down the global economic system. Ordinary Americans need government protections to ensure consumers are protected from fraud and corporate greed, to promote free and competent enterprise, to enforce environmental and safety regulations, to ensure fair and equal protections under the law for all Americans, and most importantly, to protect and defend citizens from internal and external threats to the homeland.

When most people think of government, they tend to focus solely on the Federal government, which plays a much different role in the lives of daily Americans compared to state and local governments. Non-federal government agencies ensure access to clean water, energy, sanitation, safe roads, emergency medical services, and the rule of law. Government, at every level, can only be as good as the intentions of the elected public officials who are advocating in the name of their citizens. Too many times our leaders run for public office without the best interest of the public in mind, which erodes trust of government and the intentions of public policy. My belief is that government's main focus is to protect the interest and rights of the people it serves. It should strive to promote the sustainability of its people, and to encourage the development of new industries that are independent, ethical, and innovative.

There tends to be an increased focus on the role of government in times of electoral changes and national crisis. Instead, we should always focus on how we can make government at all levels more efficient, proactive, innovative, and responsive to the needs of everyday Americans. Government should always be working side by side with private businesses and organizations alike to ensure America is consistently moving forward and developing new and innovative industries and protections for citizens and enterprise.

No one person or entity should depend on government all the time, but we must all acknowledge the need for a robust and positive government at all levels that is there to serve and protect the interest of its citizens, national and international interest. As a nation intricately involved in a global economy and network, times have greatly changed. Years ago decisions made in our own interest had no effect on other nations, now we must ensure our survival not just at home, but abroad as well. New threats, ranging from terrorism, rogue states, economic challenges in a globalized economy, the need for clean renewable energy resources, global climate change, the growth of new diseases and international pandemics, and the advent of a new knowledge based economy, are new challenges that will seek to test the ability of government and private industry alike.

The government is not some draconian entity, it is the foundation of our democracy that is made up of ordinary citizens elected by the people to serve the needs and will of the people. We shall never forget the positive power of a Democratic Republic and our own Constitutional obligations engraved in the Preamble: "We the People of the United States, in Order to form a more perfect Union, establish Justice, insure domestic Tranquility, provide for the common defense, promote the general Welfare, and secure the Blessings of Liberty to ourselves and our Posterity, do ordain and establish this Constitution for the United States of America." At its basic core the Constitution is a document dedicated to the protection and advocacy of the lives of the citizenry—putting the needs and will of the people before any other enterprise or proclamation. Our three layered system of checks and balances is not perfect by any means, but it provides an opportunity for all Americans to consistently promote the general welfare of all people and to put the interest of people above all else.

My hope is that current and future elected officials always keep in mind what is in the best interest of the people, and to consistently promote and advocate for a sustainable, innovative, and responsive government at every level that understands the need for a strong and flourishing private enterprise environment and most importantly, the interest of real everyday people.

# 6
# SEEKING A LOST GENERATION

*"Not until we are lost do we begin to understand ourselves."*
—Henry David Thoreau

You now have a full context of living an empowered and awakened life. Now it is time for you to seek others who may be lost and share with them the same ideals and tools you learned from this book. This section will challenge you to commit to building an even more prosperous, self-motivated, idealistic, self-sufficient society around your community and beyond. Each and every one of us has a role to play in empowering a lost generation. We simply need the motivation, tools, and support to know our role and to achieve at our fullest and most capable levels of success.

## Seeking a Lost Generation

As we seek to bridge the divide between past and current generations of young people and adults, there is much still to learn. Many young people feel lost, without a purpose and without hope for a better tomorrow. However, they must know that each generation has faced untold challenges, controversies, and failures. With these challenges comes the opportunity for success, prosperity, self-discovery, innovation, and idealism.

In order to truly engage and positively influence young people today, we must do more to empower them, to educate them, and to truly engage them. Young people thrive for independence, creativity, individuality, and purpose. They seek out those who will listen to them, who will help them grow, and who will guide them as they seek to influence the culture and society around them. Young people today must be challenged to think boldly and differently—and that failure is not a reason to quit, but even more reason to explore and truly understand his or her path and future in life.

In our schools where students spend a large portion of their day—we can do this with experiential learning, actively engaging, involving, and teaching our young people to be independent learners and thinkers in the 21st Century. Young people must learn to reflect on their experiences and interact in a group to solve complex problems—without fear of being "wrong". Young people must also be listened to and heard. Allowing young people to explore who they are as individuals, as leaders, as thinkers, and builders is vital for true experiential learning to take place inside and outside of the classroom.

While at home, parents must consistently and actively take a hands-on approach with their children—ensuring they are completing assigned tasks and are capable of interacting with different cultural groups and individuals who may not share the same ideals or beliefs. As young people build respect for others starting at home, they will go into a world based on the idea of embracing others who are different, not shunning or ridiculing those who are not just like them or their way of life. Parents should also seek to assist their children in their exploration and discovery of their goals and visions for life. Many children at a young age show signs of their future interests. Parents should be willing to engage their children in these activities and others to create big picture thinking and life exploration.

Communities also play a vital role in engaging and empowering a new generation of young people. Communities—which include businesses, both profit and non-profit, and leaders—must invest in a strong self-sufficient environment that embraces art, culture, education, creativity, and social independence. Communities should embrace young people and include them in different councils and policy making decisions, and economical growth and prosperity. Young people hold a wealth of ideas and creativity that should be encouraged and utilized from an early age. Teaching a new generation about hard work, independence, and the need for continued economic innovation is vital for success in the 21st Century.

I truly believe that we can engage and empower a new generation of idealistic builders, thinkers, and artists. We must be willing to learn from the youthful and energetic minds that are crying to be heard and understood.

### A New Model for Social and Education Reform

America's investment in its public education system is one of the most important issues of our generation. The reforms we take part in today will dictate whether or not we create a generation of learners, dreamers, thinkers, creators, inventors, and builders for tomorrow. We cannot continue to argue whether or not school vouchers are better than 100% public school education, if charter schools can fully prepare our young people for the real world, or if private schools are the only savior for a "real" education. Simply put, we must ensure every child is receiving a first-rate education everywhere regardless of race, belief, or social/economical upbringing. The big question then becomes, what is a first rate education? Let us start with the basics: (1) Parents who mentor and ensure their child is attending class and respecting his or her teacher; (2) Students who come prepared and willing to learn every single day and expect a challenge; and (3) Teachers and school administrators who are fully prepared, excited, and qualified to teach our next generation of leaders.

There are many examples of school systems that fail to accomplish any of those goals and there are also many who greatly match and exceed them—those are the schools we should be studying and looking at as a model for school reform and social change. We also cannot continue to endlessly throw money at schools that are simply failing our young people. There must be an end to excuses, poor results, mismanagement of resources, and failed expectations. If we expect our young people to want to learn, to be excited and able to do so, we must first offer them a product that is worthwhile and prepares them for not only the challenges of today, but for the hopes and dreams of the future. I truly believe that the future prosperity of our nation depends on the fate of our urban and rural school districts and communities alike. We must begin to truly understand these communities—meeting with parents, students, teachers, administrators, experts, and so forth, to forge ahead in a new model for education reform that directly links with a new model for social change and economic prosperity.

Young people who are engaged in their communities, who see the link between a solid education and a solid job, that believe that their home is a sacred place, that their lives are more important than drugs, gangs, or violence—these and much more are all vital in our quest to change and inspire a new generation of individuals. It will not happen over night or in a couple of years, but through the sharing of ideas and knowledge I believe we can overcome these great challenges. Through the building and linking of young people and parents with not just their school but their surrounding environment, I believe we can bring about real change. Having families create their own businesses and helping to build their own homes and schools, makes them directly responsible for their own failure or success and guides them with the necessary tools for strong financial planning, educational growth, life skills, and so forth. I believe this would be a new and interesting model for a better society for many living in poverty without hope or purpose.

We cannot simply depend on schools to do all of these things and still be able to fully educate our young people. There must be a partnership that brings together many ideas, community and business groups, and families. The investment would not only benefit those who join it, but also our society as a whole through the lessening of social welfare, reduced prison rates, violence, and drug use; instead these partnerships and reforms would create a generation of independent, self-motivated, dream-driven idealists who would create a new American legacy. When we are able to show young people a new way of opportunity who have been denied success all their life, who have been told they cannot go over the mountain, and who simply see life as a dead-end, we are able to expand on the idea that we are all in this together and that with every success story comes proof that given a challenge, a chance, and the right education, anything is possible.

We cannot continue to disregard the importance of social and economic change in our mission to reform our schools and our communities with wealth and health inequality just to name a few. These ventures and goals are all intricately linked as they feed off of one another for good or for worse. Close your eyes for a minute and imagine a community that wholeheartedly embraces its culture, its dreams and goals, its schools and leaders, and that feeds off success rather than failure, hope instead of hopelessness, prosperity over depression, and the belief that each and every one of us can control our own future, and in turn, open up new doors for a better and more enriching life. We can do this and we must or we are putting aside a whole generation of young people into the pits of failure and demise that will affect this country and this world for centuries to come. I challenge our leaders and each of us to stand up for a new model of education and community reform that embraces these ideals and beliefs:

1) Education reform is linked directly with community and social reform.

2) Empowering inner city communities to become caretakers and reformists of their own lives and neighborhoods will positively impact our nation for generations to come;

3) Increasing personal development and life skills within our communities and schools is a method to empower lasting social change;

4) Challenging all people to take positive risks and become independent entrepreneurs and leaders promotes economic growth and diversity; and

5) Failure to believe that all people are of self-worth and of vital importance to
the future success of America and the international community will only lead
to increased social welfare and dependency, lack of innovation, a stagnant
economy, and decreased independence on one's own natural gifts, ideals, and
hopes.

I know this is a broad thesis on the link between social change and education
reform, but I believe we must begin to think much broader in how we can inspire
and empower a lost generation of young people. We have watched for decades as our
society has left millions of people behind without any regard to human dignity or
support. The idea that there is this American dream for every family that wants it is
not plausible in the 21st century. We now live in a melting pot of different ideas,
beliefs, cultures, hopes, dreams, and crisis. Teaching our children with the same
methods of our parent's generation is not working.

Building more prisons, rather than solving the underlying problems of crime and
drug use, is not working. Investing in short term solutions, even with our long term
prognosis looking mediocre at best, is not working. We must begin to simply not just
think outside of the box, but tear it down. With over one million students dropping
out every year from high school, rising crime and drug rates, increased financial
instability, rising health care costs and lack of coverage, as well as changing industries
wiping out whole communities and international competition for American jobs and
college entrance slots, I am not sure there will be any American dream in ten years if
we do not start addressing the link between all of the things I wrote about earlier.

Let us not fear the future. We must see it as a rising challenge to be solved by
new minds and new ideas—let us not fear the idea that our lives are linked by the
success and failure of the least of us.

## We Must Want to Be Great

As a member of a Fraternity in my collegiate years, Sigma Phi Epsilon, and a Brother
for life, I feel empowered to think about the meaning of my time in Sig Ep and how
it has created a foundation for my life. The history of Sig Ep is broad as it was
founded in 1901 at Richmond College in Virginia by twelve young, idealistic men

who dared to be different. Sigma Phi Epsilon was founded on the belief that men must want to be great and that through this greatness they must abide by a set of founding principles that still hold true today—Virtue, Diligence, and Brotherly Love. Virtue is defined as standing for honesty and truth in all walks of life, diligence is defined as always striving for greatness through hard work and perseverance, and brotherly love is defined as the act of loving oneself first in order to truly love another.

I now know that being in Sigma Phi Epsilon while in college was truly an uplifting and spiritual experience. I learned that life is precious, that each day is a challenge that must be met and that, as a brother, I owe my nation and earth a persistent work ethic to create positive social change, so this world we call home will be better off for the next generation. I must always strive to learn, build, create, serve, help, grow, and most importantly, love. C.A. Jenkins, one of the founding brothers of the Fraternity, once wrote "the name of Sigma Phi Epsilon was born in the philosophy of love, the only foundation on which the world can have peace. This is the principle on which our Fraternity was founded."

Jenkins wrote that his founding of the Fraternity came about at his desk one evening when he fell asleep and began to dream. He dreamed of an earth filled with death, hate, destruction, and unhappiness, in which he saw "ten hundred thousand monuments to the newly dead soldiers of the earth." He asked the Recording Angel why this was happening and what it meant. The Angel responded "Men have failed to understand the simple teachings of the Prince of the Earth." Jenkins awoke from his dream wondering exactly what this meant to him and his future. As he slept for the night he dreamed again, but this time he saw a world filled with happiness, children walking to school, people singing, churches filled with people, and "the nations of the earth were at peace, every nation with its brother nation."

Lastly, he asked the Angel what brought this change on the earth and "the Angel of God" pointed Jenkins to a passage of Scripture: Matthew 22:37-40. *Thou shalt love the Lord thy God with all thy heart, and with all thy soul, and with all thy mind. This is the first and great commandment. And the second is like unto it, 'Thou shalt love thy neighbor as thyself.'*" This passage created the core foundation of Sigma Phi Epsilon: love. If we all truly care for one another and love one another like true brothers, peace will be the resulting effect.

Through love we gain understanding, power, trust, and the ability to live a life based on the care and concern of the least of us. When someone asks me why I joined a fraternity, I can tell them it was not about me, it was about you and everyone else. I am here to serve, to make the world a better place through the betterment of myself and my fellow man. All of our lives should be a beacon of hope, idealism, and prosperity for the rest of the world to replenish from. We shall be the leaders of today, tomorrow, and forever. And we must always stay true to our ideals and values, because through these core values we will be better people and will truly change the world.

## Creating a New Era of Educational Excellence

Recent studies have shown that the historic No Child Left Behind Act, which aimed to improve the measuring and performance of schools across the nation primarily based on standardized test scores, has failed in its attempt to challenge students and close the achievement gap between minority and white students[2]. Today in our country, students are taught and trained to pass a test all year long as if they are cars on an assembly line, unable to discover, imagine, or create. However, not every school is a failure as there are many excellent public, private, and charter schools in America, but sadly not enough. Having worked in the Washington, DC public school system, by far one of the worst in the nation has truly shown me how much our nation and education system has failed at the monumental task of preparing our young people for the challenges of the 21$^{st}$ Century.

Some blame the teachers and many blame school administrators for their inability to reorganize and retool our society for the challenges of the future. For far too long we have seen students as the problem, more so than the solution. We blame them when they fail, we force them to take standardized tests to compete against other students nationwide, and we do not allow them to partake in self-discovery and tap into their intellectual curiosity. Education and learning is not a race, it is a journey. Something that I learned very quickly in my classroom is that no matter how good or bad a student performs on a test, when you truly sit down with them in a small group or one-on-one meeting and talk with them, mentor them, and allow them to explore new thoughts and ideas, they always exceed expectations. Kids of today do not like when they are forced to think alike, write alike, or do anything alike. Each child is special and has a unique talent or gift, favorite subject, and style of learning.

---

[2] http://www.nytimes.com/2009/04/29/education/29scores.html

It simply then becomes the teachers' job to allow and facilitate their students exploration of their hopes and dreams, goals, and educational standards. The classroom should be an incubator for educational exploration, acceptance, individuality, and creativity. When students are given meaningful assignments that match their intellectual talents and critically challenge them to think outside of the box to create their own assignments under the guidance of their teachers, we will be proud of the resulting successes. These standards of individual exploration and critical thinking development must be known in the classroom and pursued everyday with every child. Students of all educational abilities should be intertwined with one another to challenge all them to push themselves academically.

Teachers should be hired on the basis of intelligence, their love for learning and children, ability to motivate and inspire, and ability to reach their students in a meaningful and powerful way. There must be high standards of success and continued development for teachers, and an emphasis on recruiting and retaining the best and brightest minds for our young people, because they deserve nothing less. In order for America to turn the page on its abhorrent failure to adequately educate and inspire every child that strives for excellence and success, we must begin anew, admit our mistakes, and start over. We cannot expect success teaching our students in schools that reign from the 1960's and curricula that ignores the challenges of our new global economy. I truly believe that it is not too late. We may not be able to save every child, but we must try and we must start now, because our future depends on it.

If we start believing in our youth and we develop a new model for teaching and learning, standardized testing would be obsolete and we will know that we have succeeded by increased graduation rates and college enrollment, economic output, and so forth. We know what must be done, we know how to teach children and it is important to remember that these changing times require new and innovative ways of teaching, learning, and inspiration. We must create a new mark of educational excellence that embraces students as the solution, starting a new beginning of self-worth, self-discovery, and imagination.

## Generation Y: How the Creativity of Millennials
## Can Change the Work Place and the World

The job search has begun, constant Internet searching and a review of contacts opens some leads, and the perfect job is right around the corner. Now it is time to find that dream company that has a position that fits you just right. As a millennial and young employee in the 21$^{st}$ Century, I am constantly thinking of how inefficient, disorganized, non tech-savvy, and mundane some employers can be. Many young people today see their place of employment as an extension of who they are and the ideas they hold for the present and their futures. Many ask themselves, "Is this job going to lead me to a higher paid position?", "does my company pay for graduate school?", "do my co-workers listen to my ideas and opinions?", and "do I come in everyday feeling as though I am making a positive difference?"

I am sure there are hundreds of questions that go through the minds of those young workers under the age of thirty. Our generation has been raised on the idea that we can achieve anything we put our minds to, that technology is our friend, and that multi-tasking is the norm. We hold ourselves to high standards when it comes to setting goals and achieving them, and we expect those around us to treat us as equals regardless of age or educational background. The old school idea of a top-down work structure does not bode well in our minds. We view the work place as a bottom-up structure where we are able to create positive change every single day without having to deal with red tape and four different executive officers for approval. If we have a great idea for a new product or service we expect to be heard!

Another vital characteristic of our generation involves efficiency. Wasting time in a two hour meeting with no agenda where nothing is accomplished is never a positive moment. Older generations are used to a regular eight hour or more workweek, where even if they have completed assigned tasks or have nothing to do, it is the norm to stay in the office anyways. This is considered a complete waste of time for younger generations. After a certain point it becomes quite depressing to sit in an office space with nothing to do and then to be assigned mundane tasks to simply waste time.

Young employees also view the need for independence and time to decompress throughout the day. Employers that offer yoga, gyms, cafeterias, lounges, etc. allow young employers to relax and refresh their minds. Many companies that are voted best workplaces for young people such as Google and Microsoft are all known to have built their work place structures around the habits of Generation Y. When employers invest in the lifestyles of young people and their employees in general, they see much greater benefits in the workplace and productivity. Young employees also strive to make big changes in a short period to time. This means employers must allow their young millennial workers to design meaningful projects and tasks that will have a real impact on the company. Mixing in social awareness and volunteer programs is also a positive step in the right direction, as our generation has been built on the idea of giving back, making a positive difference in the lives of others, and social change.

Communication is also a vital aspect to connecting with Generation Y. Younger workers, even with all of their technology use, are quite personable. They expect a fast-paced communication stream from phone, e-mail, web conferencing, and any other form of communication that diversifies team work and openness. If workers are capable of working from home once a week with these and other communication means, this would greatly impact the work style of younger workers and the company as a whole. Young people have no problem working from home and are quite used to it, especially with the advent of online courses and assignments. The typical brick and mortar cubical workplace is not conducive to how young people work efficiently. Give them the opportunity to go outside the office and mingle with clients and attend conferences. The more engaged you can keep young employees the more chance you have of retaining them and motivating them to become great innovators within your organization.

Those under thirty also have a deep belief in their abilities, accomplishments, and visions for success. When they feel as though they are trusted and their company supports and believes in them this will pay huge dividends in the long run as trust is vital to build a strong employee-employer relationship. We see the world as our playing ground and we intend to shape it with or without a corporation leading the way. Entrepreneurship and especially social entrepreneurship, have both created a new era of business development, that along with the Internet and social networking, has a created a huge swelling of young people becoming quite successful at a young age.

Many young workers see their time working for a company as a means to further their own creative ambitions in hopes of running their own business one day. And with the Internet and social networking, it is easier for young people to find similar people who hold the same ideas and interests to create their own entrepreneurial dreams. Although the forty year plan of working with one company and retiring is over, the hard work and innovative talents of our generation will reap major dividends in quite a short period of time, as long as employers are willing to accommodate the new work styles of Generation Y.

And lastly, we should not forget about performance management. Young workers take pride in excelling at a high level and achieving set goals and objectives. Ensure that these goals young employees are working on are both measurable and purposeful. Rather than criticizing, encourage and ensure young employees are given the adequate tools and resources to achieve their work plans and mentor them along the way. Many organizations are used to pulling in employees for a quick twenty minute evaluation on his or her work performance; however, this approach has to be updated. Instead of micro-managing from afar, the use of constant communication, team work, and observation of projects so employees are constantly gaining input throughout the process, decreases the need for a twice a year review of an employee's work. Young employees will see this as a means for growth and development, instead of a mere attack of his or her perceived mistakes or imperfections.

Generation Y truly is an inspired, motivated, idealistic, and creative workforce. Employers should do more to reach out to this untapped group, where constant thinking and innovative abilities far outweigh the risks. Creating a corporate culture that embraces who Generation Y is will reap major benefits in the short and long-term for company growth. The challenges of our ever growing global economy will only become fiercer and greater, which is why now we should tap into the power of Generation Y.

## History is On the Side of Progress: Where Do You Stand?

Once in a generation we all face pivotal and monumental questions that err on the side of progress and freedom or stalemate and regress. Where each of us ends up is the story of life and opportunity. We may not agree on all of the issues of social progress and our reasons for or against may be ions apart. However, one thing we can all agree on is that history does not lie in the sands of time and those who stand for progress and freedom are on the right side of history. How we each decide our opinions and beliefs on vital issues in this lifetime may be for many reasons: our own life experiences, family upbringing, spiritual and religious beliefs, or just our own inklings and understandings. Everyone is entitled to their own ideals and beliefs without being thrown to the sidelines and beaten because of them. However, when those opportunities come along once in a generation and we must each choose a side to take and the part of history to be on, it is a very difficult choice for all of us.

Monumental issues of our time such as slavery, social security, Medicare, civil rights, and health care are some of the most defining issues of progress and humanity in our generation. Many people fought dearly and with a righteous spirit to bring about positive social change in this country that was and still is needed today. When the Thirteenth Amendment passed in 1865 and brought slavery to an end it was an amazing triumph for America. The belief that all people were to be treated as human beings that lived and breathed the same air, and shared the same hopes and dreams past and present was paramount for a new, more just America. It took debate, it took compromise, and most importantly, it took the will and desire to change course and see that progress for thousands of people was a positive outcome for our country. So many people gave their lives and their reputations in a time where bucking against the status quo was not only hard politically and socially, but deadly.

As our nation continued to progress and understand the notion of true liberty, freedom, and prosperity for all its people, the idea that some of our most vulnerable citizens and senior citizens could become homeless, unemployed, or simply be forced to work for life without a sense of financial or a social safety-net, the Social Security Act was signed into law by President Roosevelt in 1935. When it was first created it was not a perfect system by any means. African-Americans and women were mostly excluded as well as a good portion of blue-collar and domestic workers. However, overtime numerous amendments and changes were made to the act bringing more people into the program, increases in benefits, and many more changes that created a program that has defined the social and financial well-being of millions of hard-working Americans.

Our leaders began to see that we had not made enough progress in terms of providing for our most helpless citizens, sadly due to the fact that medical benefits were left out of the initial Social Security Act of 1935. Many credit Medicare as the first national health program for Americans. Signed into law in 1965 by President Lyndon Johnson, Medicare was as vital then as it is today in ensuring the opportunity for millions to visit a professional doctor and receive the medical care every human deserves as they age and lose the ability to earn an acceptable wage. Our nation during its growth has realized the importance of humility and compassion in terms of providing for our most vulnerable citizens. The idea that what makes us human is our ability to put ourselves in the shoes of others who are in need and to not just stand and watch, but to provide a real sense of security and opportunity is one of America's most prominent and lasting cornerstones of justice and equality that many nations envy.

Even with the passage of many of these pieces of legislation and acts, there was still a huge segment of the population that was excluded from these programs and the benefits thereof: African-Americans. Left in the darkness of progress and the trails of history, African-Americans were still living a separate and truly un-equal lifestyle upheld by the United States Government. Many national, local, and state officials did not believe the Constitution or any legal document applied to the tribulations and struggles of the African-American community. If it was not for the fight and struggle that so many African-Americans and many whites put up to integrate colored people into the American society, America, even in all of its glory, would never have truly stood the test of freedom, opportunity, or social justice. Leaders such as Rosa Parks, Martin Luther King, Jr., Malcolm X, Lyndon B. Johnson, John F. Kennedy, A. Philip Randolph, John Lewis, and so many others fought to open the doors of justice for African-Americans that for far too long were slammed shut. Freedom marches, the de-segregation of schools and public places, the right to vote, sit-ins, peaceful and non-peaceful protests, and much more all led to a revolution in truly freeing African-Americans from the bondage of modern day slavery.

In our time, we must stand for a history of social justice and opportunity. We face many issues that will define not just the lives of Americans today, but of future generations for decades to come. We face similar challenges and calls for equal opportunity, social justice, hope, and progress that many of our Founding Fathers and past generations fought so dearly to create and provide for the least of us today. Many see, including me, the fight for affordable and comprehensive health insurance for all Americans as our generations call for social progress and opportunity. In a nation that spends over $2.2 trillion a year on health care, nearly twice what other developed nation's spend, with over 40 million Americans without any insurance, not including those who are under-insured, many Americans are being left behind and our nation's long-term fiscal stability and health safety net will continue to deteriorate. Some 60% of all bankruptcies in America are caused by the inability to pay for health care expenses. There are many who argue that the status-quo is acceptable, that allowing millions of Americans to roam freely without the ability to pay for the rising costs of health care in the richest country is acceptable. Opponents of universal health care promote the idea that millions who are left without medical insurance is acceptable and unrelated to the broader economic success of America. This is unacceptable in terms of our nation's fiscal outlook and more importantly, America's call to social justice and opportunity for all citizens of this nation.

No one should have to go homeless because they cannot afford their health care bill or because they are under insured. Our nation's very own social fabric hangs in the balance based on our own faithfulness and call to serve to those who are the most vulnerable. There are those who argue our nation's legislative branch does not have the Constitutional authority to pass a comprehensive health reform bill. The United States Constitution is a legal framework on which our country was founded that created three branches of government, among other vital rights and expectations, to carry out the will of the people. The Constitution created the limitations of power through checks and balances and gave authority to the legislative branch for all law-making purposes. If our Founding Fathers sat out to dictate every single law, program, or idea past and present of which our leaders could or could not debate, propose, and/or pass within the legal limits of a three-branch government, the Constitution itself would have failed to acknowledge the power of change and the voice of the people in a representative democracy over the course of its history. Those who support President Obama's health care legislation are right in their use of the Commerce Clause to defend mandated health insurance.

The Preamble itself is clear that our Founding Fathers did not seek to implement such rigid outlook, but sought to provide guiding principles by which our leaders should govern and adhere to a representative system of governance: "We the People of the United States, in Order to form a more perfect Union, establish Justice, insure domestic Tranquility, provide for the common defense, promote the general Welfare, and secure the Blessings of Liberty to ourselves and our Posterity, do ordain and establish this Constitution for the United States of America." The Preamble is quite clear in that it is not seeking to mandate nor restrict the ability of future generations within the confines of a legal framework to determine their own destiny. Quite the contrary to the arguments of those who seek to use the Constitution when they disagree with the legal authority of our legislative branch to create policies it sees fit to progress social welfare and the tranquility of our society, the Constitution wholeheartedly embraces the ideals of justice, progress, opportunity, and the defense of not just our country, but also the social fabric of our culture.

There is no way to ever know how our Founding Fathers would vote or react to the great expansion of our society in terms of equal opportunity and social justice for so many that in their day were simply slaves to the whips of injustice and hopelessness. However, I strongly believe that they would be proud that our country has come so far in its preservation of a free society that within itself has broken down the barriers of hate, tyranny, and the shackles of oppression. When I take a look in the mirror every single day I think about how many still suffer in a society in which even in our darkest hours is plentiful of wealth and opportunity for so many.

We may not always see it, believe in it, or even know it is available, but what I do know is when history is written in the tablets of time and those who come after us turn the pages of our generation's greatest challenges, I want them to see a people that were humble, free, loving, hopeful, and most importantly, standing up for progress and positive social change. They will know the trials and tribulations of our past, the opportunities of our present, and our hopes for the future. That even in our darkest days, we always stood on the side of opportunity not stalemate, hope not fear, and opportunity over injustice.

## The Promise of Humanity

There are many people who believe that America should not have given funds to Haiti and other impoverished nations in their times of need during our own tough times and struggles of economic calamity and recovery. There are those who argue that there is no similarity between America's own struggle as the richest country in the world to provide health care for all of its citizens and our quest to relieve the pain and suffering of millions throughout the world. However, I respectfully disagree and offer strong support behind the idea that we are all inextricably linked to the promise of humanity. The stronger and healthier society we can build here at home, the more we can go out and make the world a better place. I wish to not make this a political issue or argument, but a human argument in all that we do and fight for, not only internationally, but here at home. The promise that we are all in this together, that suffering on the streets of Haiti is the same as suffering on the streets of Detroit. As human beings that are intelligently designed to feel pain, to feel hope, to love, to care, to cry, to save, to have faith in one another, and ultimately to live out the promise of humanity in all that we do no matter if it is in our own backyard or in a foreign land—we are all called to a quest greater than ourselves.

The belief that seeing the suffering of children and families who are our own flesh and blood, even if we did not cause it, even if we could not prevent it, even if we do not know those in pain, our own innate soul tells us that it is not right and that we must act, is a strong bond of humanity. If the resources, equipment, and technology are available to relieve human suffering to further our quest for the promise of humanity, then we shall act. Simply standing in the darkness of a corner or changing the channel or refusing to look at the newspaper headlines will not make the horrors of destruction disappear; we still know that suffering is happening all around and we know that our souls tells us that we must do more to address the loss of humanity.

Even if you refuse to give your money, time, or even prayers, know that in your own life in times of strife, pain and suffering, there will always be someone, somewhere fighting for you who is lifting your spirits in his or her heart, volunteering in your honor, and holding out faith that the promise of humanity shall not just extend in times of destruction and despair, but also in times of happiness, joy, and success. The idea that good health is vital to a successful life no matter if you are in Africa or America, the fight will never end and the light of hope and justice shall always shine in your corner, that even though there will be doubters, naysayers, and many unwilling to commit their own resources to your needs, there will be many willing to do the opposite. Live out your life in support of justice, hope, love, and most importantly: The Promise of Humanity.

## Creating a Great Organization in the 21st Century

We have all heard the cliché, "behind every great company, are great employees" or something close to that—maybe great customers, who knows. What is quite important and unique to great companies such as SAS, Google, Microsoft, Facebook, Apple, DreamWorks Animation, and many others, is that they listen to the needs of not only their customers, but their employees. Needs that may not always be spoken, but make it possible for employees to work in the best possible environment in a time in which many spend more hours in the office than at home. When employees feel respected, appreciated, and know that the work they are accomplishing is directly and positively influencing the end consumer, morale goes up. For instance, look at SAS, a privately held software company, actually the largest in the world. They have had only one CEO in their thirty four years of existence. Not only is it a very profitable company, it is quite stable and has fared very well in even the toughest of economic downturns and the tech boom and bust years.

SAS is known for treating its employees with the utmost respect, providing an on-site day care service, a health center, cafeteria, a gym and basketball courts, massage therapy, and so much more! Their guiding principles are simple: "If you treat employees as if they make a difference, they will make a difference" and "Satisfied employees create satisfied customers." Many companies have taken this lead, whether or not due to the success of SAS, it is a good thing overall. Google and

Facebook, two companies that epitomize the youthful, energetic, and employee-centered lifestyle, are what many see as the gold standard for the future of not just the business world, but government. Many of these companies hire top consultants to design the workspace in a manner that allows employees to thrive, breathe better, foster teamwork, and creativity with walls that are erasable whiteboards.

When you look at Generation Y, those typically under thirty, this generation craves companies that respect their own individual identity, work styles, and communication methods. Many young people today crave companies that match their ideals, beliefs, and views on society and their visions of the world. There was a time when many people worked because they had to or because they felt obligated to work for forty years for the same company then retire happily ever after. However, that is no longer the case as it is not strange for younger workers today to have had two or three different employers within four years after college.

With many baby boomers working later into their golden years, there will be an inevitable clash of generations in the workplace that will test the limits of technological and social communication that many members of Generation Y are used to and comfortable with. How companies bring these two generations together will be pivotal in ensuring a seamless (or close to it) transition from a more stable workforce to a very transient one where employees no longer feel obligated to stay connected with a company for twenty or forty years. Younger workers are also more likely to challenge the workplace culture and how the company interacts and treats its employees. Generation Y was raised to believe that speaking up and fighting for positive change was as much a right as getting a full social security retirement check is to baby boomers. With all of these forces coming together the challenges will be different and multi-faceted. How each company and government agency handles this barrage of changes and employee dynamics will be quite important to developing a workforce and social apparatus that works and creates those satisfied employees and customers that SAS has so elegantly done over the last thirty plus years.

Companies that aim to improve the quality of life for their employees will be better off in the short and long term. If companies want to empower their employees they must provide the resources and opportunities to create a more dynamic and open workplace where employees enjoy the work they are doing, feel challenged, and feel as though their talents and gifts are being fully utilized and rewarded. Professional development is vital in the workplace because it constantly revitalizes employees and prepares them for the challenges of not just the present, but the future. As our economy changes, so will the tools and needs of employees on a daily basis. When companies communicate actively, fully, and openly with employees, a real level of trust is developed where employees feel free, engaged, and able to voice their concerns, ideas, hopes, and fears.

Organization workshops, events, and presentations all help to open the hearts and minds of employees so they feel directly and intricately linked to the success or failure of the organization. Having a fair and open evaluation system is vital, so employees are rewarded for success and growth and further developed and provided new opportunities to learn and excel as a means to create a cycle of rejuvenation and leadership opportunities. Lastly, organizations, both large and small, must do more to create an environment in which employees enjoy and love coming to work every day, where they know their employer trusts them and believes in their abilities to bring about positive and influential change.

It is important that employers constantly evaluate who they are, what they are attempting to accomplish, and how to ensure employees are always a part of that cycle. This will not only create a more open, diverse, and enjoyable workplace, but overtime it will create a product that customers also love, believe in, and appreciate. Customers and their feelings tend to be a great system of measurement of how employees are not just performing, but most importantly, how they are being treated.

### Putting Purpose Back into Education: Engaging Young People

In order to truly achieve success in our efforts to reform the education bureaucracy we must empower students, families, and teachers alike to take control of their own destinies. School districts across the country have spent millions of dollars purchasing new educational programs, expert advice, materials, and systems, but at the end of the day, if these ideas and programs are not supported from the bottom up they will not succeed. Students must believe in themselves, set goals, and vigorously work towards them. Parents must ensure their kids are learning and that they hold high expectations for their child's school and educational processes. Schools and teachers alike must listen to the needs of each student, set high educational standards that are measurable, and consistently preach a message of success and opportunity to each student.

The message we send our students, the resources we provide them to achieve their dreams and goals, and the standards in which we hold each and every student to must exceed all expectations. No child should be deemed a failure due to a lack of opportunity. Every school should be preparing students for life after graduation— whether it is work or college. When we build an educated and fully capable population we will put our country on course with other developed nations in the world, specifically in math and science. However, that does not mean we should only focus on those two subjects. It is vital to ensure our students are receiving a balanced and diverse course load in school that allows each and every one of them to explore literature, music, history, language, and culture—just to name a few. This is the United States of America—we can surely do better and we owe it to this generation and future generations more opportunities to excel and succeed in the 21st Century.

We currently have a situation where "only six in ten children from low-income families can expect to graduate from high school and only one in three will enroll in college and only one in seven will earn a bachelor's degree[3]"— we are failing our young people.

When "more than 12 million students are projected to drop out over the next decade that will cost the nation $3 trillion[4]"—we are failing our young people. And ultimately, at the end of the day as we continue to under invest in our failing schools and our disadvantaged communities, we are failing our nation. We can and must do more to notice the signs of a troubled student at a young age before it is too late. We know from research that attendance and course performance in the early years of a student's life can predict failure or success down the road.

We know that when a student feels empowered and in control of his or her own destiny he or she is more likely to succeed and do better in school. If a student is not motivated to learn or feel as though education today has no purpose for his or her future he or she will not learn. We must do more to develop and engage our young people in terms of leadership and self-development. Once we realize that quality instruction, curricula, and resources must match the goals and expectations that our young people hold for themselves and what we expect from them, we can then realize that there is much more work to do and each day must be a march towards a bigger vision. I believe there is time, but as the days, weeks, and years go by our objectives must be clear, broad, ambitious, measurable, and above all, diverse and equal.

---

[3] Bedsworth, W., Colby, S., & Doctor, J. (2006). *Reclaiming the American Dream.* Boston, MA: Bridgespan
[4] City Year

### Economic Opportunity and Sustainability Key
### to Bridging the Great Wealth Divide

The dramatic wealth gap between people of color and those who are white is one of the most troubling and emerging social and economic issues of our time. In an era where economic prosperity is becoming harder to attain than ever before, it is even more of a climb for people of color. We need to bring together business, government, profit/non-profit groups, educational institutions, and individuals to devise new solutions to increase economic wealth and achievement across the color spectrum. This system must not merely be focused on handouts, but educating those within disadvantaged communities and populations about the resources and tools available to them to become more economically and socially sustainable citizens.

We must devise new strategies to reach those who have been left in the shadows. Strategies that are not built on animosity, jealousy, or hate, but on the reality that we all succeed when the least of us achieve. Creating economic policies and programs that lift people out of poverty and free from government programs into the light of prosperity, independence, and sustainable economic growth is the challenge of our generation. According to a recent study by Brandeis University, "White families typically have assets worth $100,000, up from $22,000 in the mid-1980s. African-American families' assets stand at just $5,000, up from around $2,000."(1).

Wealth allows families to save, retire happy, pay off debts, invest in educational opportunities, start a new business, and to leave funds for future generations. Every American deserves the opportunity to the pursuit of happiness and to help build a strong America now and in the future. For far too long the playing field has been very much skewed towards those with wealth—either passed down from generations or recently acquired. Special tax privileges/shelters, loan and investment programs, and institutional policies have unfairly left out middle and low income Americans of all races and ethnicities.

Economic opportunity should not only be for those that are already privileged, but also those who seek a new life and ultimately control over their own economic destiny. For most people of color, equal opportunity was not legal until after the 1960s. Through a host of boycotts, protests, and legal victories, people of color ultimately gained the opportunity to become integrated into American society. Before then, generations of parents and grandparents were never able to create or gain wealth through business ownership, investing, savings, or any means of economic sustainability. With the passage of numerous pieces of Civil Rights legislation, most thought that equal opportunity was on the horizon, however, many states, businesses, and government institutions still refused to follow through on the integration of those who had been left behind in American culture.

Here we are today; fifty plus years since the legal fight for equal opportunity for all groups, and many communities face the same issues of economic viability and sustainability as their forefathers. Disadvantaged communities face high incarceration rates, a lack of educational opportunities, decreased wealth, a lack of home ownership, bad credit, no savings, low wage jobs, and a cycle of poverty that rivals some third-world nations. If I could sum up the issues facing disadvantaged people it would simply be: we can do better! Simply blaming others for the myriad of issues and problems facing the economically challenged ignores our own responsibility to improve our own lives and that of future generations who will come after us. Structural issues within our society are still here today that reach educationally, economically, and socially. However, we must continue to overcome these obstacles, no matter how wide, deep, or encompassing they may seem—we shall overcome.

It is never too late to spin the wheels of hope and opportunity. It is never too late to use the past as a motivation for the future. It is never too late to seek out new opportunities of prosperity and equality. Our time on this earth is short, our days are numbered, which is why we must use every waking second of every single day to fight for not only our present, but our future. The issue of wealth inequality in America is not just a black issue, a Hispanic issue, or a white issue; ultimately, it is an America issue. Yes, minority groups are disproportionately represented in the bottom of the wealth divide, but ultimately America suffers socially, structurally and economically, both here and abroad, due to the expanding income divide. When we leave out a whole segment of our population in the quest to live the American dream, we are failing to improve America's short and long term social and economical development needs here at home.

We must move on this issue from every angle, while at the same time being cognizant of how the issue is presented, debated, and solved. People of all ages, races, beliefs, and cultures must be invited to this conversation so we can work together as a nation to not just create a new level of trust and opportunity for a class of people, but to build up a generation of our society that has been left out for far too long. The quest to create a bigger pool of opportunity for those who seek to earn it should always be the main objective. As we work with organizations, businesses, individuals, and government agencies alike, we must do more to discover not only the causes and repercussions of income and wealth inequality, but also create workable solutions that are comprehensive and sustainable. Martin Luther King Jr. wrote this in a letter from a Birmingham City Jail: *"We must come to see that human progress never rolls in on wheels of inevitability...We must use time creatively, and forever realize that the time is always ripe to do right."*

We must answer four important questions to start a dialogue and begin to develop real, actionable solutions:

A) What kind of programs can we develop to bridge the wealth gap?

B) How can all sectors of America's economy (business, government, non-profit groups, individuals, etc.) become involved to intervene in this crisis and provide sustainable solutions?

C) What sort of conferences/round-tables/discussions can we hold to solve wealth inequality?

D) What does the data tell us about people of color and the effects of decreased opportunity—educationally, economically, and socially, due to the wealth gap? What are the causes/outcomes?

E) What is the root causes of economic inequality?

1) A $95,000 question: why are whites five times richer than blacks in the US? http://www.guardian.co.uk/world/2010/may/17/white-people-95000-richer-black

Please review the summary and full study released by the Institute on Assets and Social Policy at Brandeis University via http://www.brandeis.edu/now/2010/may/wealthgaprelease.html

## Live What You Imagine

I love to imagine a world that is designed and lived by idealistic, thoughtful, outgoing, and imaginative individuals that fear not what is in the unknown, but embrace it. A world that consistently values diversity of thought, ideas, cultures, and people is what I imagine. A place that never ceases to challenge us in all of our endeavors, that pushes us to our limits, both mentally and physically, and that builds a sustainable environment that bears witness to our love of humanity, nature, and quality of life. Just think for a moment about the opportunities that so many of us have missed out on or simply rejected out of fear, spite, jealousy, or our own disillusionment with what is possible. Instead, our basis for living should be defined not by the length of our longevity on this earth or the accolades that are bestowed upon us, but by our spirit of exploration and ingenuity to make a positive difference, not just in the lives of others, but for future generations and for the planet itself.

Living out our dreams, realizing the true potential in each of us to make real positive sustainable social change, and our ability to reconcile our differences and own selfish vices to see that a life lived fully for the advancement of others and society is a right and responsibility we are all privileged to. No one is perfect and we all have our faults and failures; however, those should not be viewed as weaknesses, but learning tools that will help strengthen the resolve, optimism, and path to which each of us seeks to travel on. The paths are uniquely different, but a journey nonetheless. The power and spirit of the human mind and soul are like none other and cannot be replicated in a lab or even in the likeness of another person. We are so very different, but at the same time each of our abilities to love one another, to care for one another, to believe in something greater than our individual selves, and the idea that ordinary people are capable of doing extraordinary things, are quite enduring and universal.

I have always believed that it is never too late to live a life worth dreaming of. Even in times of darkness, discouragement, confusion, and failure there is always a light worth heading towards. Dreams and visions are not meant to simply stay imaginary and wishful, they are meant to be explored and lived out. Knocking down barriers and living your destiny is a challenge worth taking. Always remember that the prosperity of future generations depends on the actions of those before it to create a society that upholds a system of values and expectations built on a foundation of opportunity, a spirit of generosity, creativity, and imagination.

## Crayons and Paper: Exploring the Endless Bounds of Creativity

Growing up having just a couple of crayons and a blank piece of notebook paper rivals our use of laptops and smart phones for instant gratification and creative expression today. Instead of drawing, we are blogging or tweeting or on Facebook, among a myriad of other technologically creative tools. Maybe even our definition of creativity has changed from the idea that we are all capable of creating and developing new ideas and processes to simply finding those we have accepted to be the creative type. And by this, I mean we only expect certain kids to exhibit creative behavior instead of developing it or employers look at the same universities for creative talent instead of broadening their search. In a recent poll by IBM, some 1,500 CEO's chose creativity as the No. 1 "leadership competency" of years to come. The importance of creative thinking and problem solving is not just vital for the future economic growth and competitiveness for many nations, including America, but also to the development of new products, services, and solutions to complex problems.

The way a school's curriculum interacts with and challenges students is vital to building up the creative juices in young people. Education cannot just be about memorization of facts and numbers, standardized testing, and clustering kids into defined intelligence groups; it must also be about developing and challenging the creative IQ of kids all across socioeconomic boundaries. Guiding students to not just answer a question, but to determine its implications, new solutions, and to grasp a well-rounded understanding of complex problems should be expected of every child. It is also vital to allow students to have their own creative bubble of exploration: the ability for students to create their own projects, discover their purpose, and ultimately to develop their own life's niche.

We live in such a fast-paced society where the integration of technology and information are both testing the boundaries of how we educate our children and what we expect them to learn for their own future potential. I suspect the best way for us to do this without interfering with each child's own personal creative prerogative and development is to provide equal resources and most importantly, time, so they too can live their own dreams and individual identities. And this does not mean guidance and support should be thrown out the door, quite the contrary—young people need guidance and support to nurture their ideas and creative juices.

Expanding the creative resources and opportunities for young people is the main priority, but it is also important for adults. Allowing workers to explore their talents and creative abilities in an open environment not only improves employee morale, but also opens new doors for the employer in terms of product development and idea generation. Challenging both young people and adults to be creative thinkers is not only vital for the short term needs of our society, but also the long term prospects for our nation and for many others.

In your spare time think of a problem that needs a solution, research information on the problem, possible causes, find out what has worked, what has not worked, what can be improved, and why/how; then come up with possible ideas and solutions to the problem, picking out the ones that are most feasible and effective; lastly, create a plan to implement your idea, putting all the pieces of the puzzle together. The human brain can be the most inquisitive instrument at our disposal to create new solutions to old and new problems, and to unleash the creative juices within us. We should no longer accept that being different is out of the norm, but instead see uniqueness as a quality to be admired and fostered. Maybe we all could use just a couple of crayons and a blank piece of paper to once again reignite our creative sparks.

## Generation We Solve: Creating a Sustainable Society

The challenges we face are many, ranging from the development of new life-saving drugs to the reforming of our stale education system to creating a more sustainable environment. These new and old challenges will require a new way of thinking, creative solutions, and more opportunities for those who have been left out of our society for too long to get into the mix. I believe there are a number of opportunities by which we can bring about revolutionary and vital change to improve the social, economic, and global well-being and longevity of our civilization.

Firstly, through the development of sustainable communities we can begin to plant the seeds for positive change. Typically, when someone thinks of a sustainable community they think of clean water, shelter, food, and the ability of its residents to fend for themselves on a daily basis. Those are necessities for sustainability, but we must go much deeper structurally and socially. Sustainable communities must have a strong economic structure that allows for people to start their own businesses and to cultivate positive relationships through partnerships with community and business organizations. The more local businesses, the more people feel connected to the products and services being produced, therefore creating a more sustainable and growing local populace. In order to create this environment, both the public and private sector must work together to create a positive environment for sustainable growth. This can occur through pro-business policies, monitoring mechanisms to prevent fraud and abuse, educational programs to educate and empower ordinary citizens to become entrepreneurs, and a constant discussion on what communities can do to always improve and grow in an environmentally and economically sustainable way.

Secondly, education is vital to ensuring not just a short term solution to creating a sustainable community, but for long-term economic output and development. The more opportunities all people, especially young people, have to learn, develop, create, and to think independently and constructively the more likely they will be able to invest in the short and long-term goals of any given society, both locally, nationally, and globally. A great education cannot just be reserved for a select few or those who are privileged to live in wealthy neighborhoods. The more educated our society is, the more economic growth and development we as a people see on a national and global scale. Education also opens doors for people who come from low-income socioeconomic backgrounds as it provides an escape from the claws of poverty and destitute living. When people feel they have an opportunity to live their dreams and to play a positive role in society, they are less likely to turn to gangs, drugs, and prison. We must build an education system that values a diverse thought of ideas, talents, and creativity.

Lastly, we must embrace creative thinking and being different as a means to encourage new ideas and processes. For far too long, those who think different or come up with the most out of the box ideas are those who tend to be ignored or pushed to the side, both in business and government. We need to cultivate and encourage a culture that embraces a diversity of thoughts, ideas, and solutions. The challenges we face are only becoming more complex and unique, therefore we must be open to new ways of thinking and embrace a new generation of thought and creativity that not only develops new systems and processes, but builds upon what works throughout science, education, energy, technology, manufacturing, business, and government. There is so much hope and promise on this earth with many endless possibilities, but we must do better at harnessing the visionary thoughts of not only those who are older, but of young people as well. The ability to solve complex problems is not just the cause of a few, but of many. We must empower our students, teachers, parents, leaders, and individual citizens to develop their own unique roles in society and to actively pursue their dreams and goals.

The present and future success of our society as we know it depends on all of us sharing in the ups and downs, good and bad, positives and negatives, because we are all in this together. We must do more to make systems more efficient, practical, useful, sustainable, and transferable. And this in no way means that independent thinking and success should somehow be automatically shared with others, but when you build a sustainable, creative, and diverse society, success becomes ingrained and expected. People are more willing to support social causes, invest in economic development, and improve the social structures within their communities. The fact is we are all capable of doing more together than we are apart. Lifting up communities both here at home and abroad economically, creating clean energy, promoting renewed research and science education in our secondary schools, and believing in the power of positive and sustainable social change shall be our cause, and it is my belief that the millennial generation can blaze this trail of development, opportunity, and idealism.

## Open Your Mind to the Power of Knowledge

Information truly does flow at the speed of sound. Through the power of the Internet and an even more interconnected world, the ability to search and find the necessary information one seeks is more plentiful than ever before. However, there is still much to be discussed on how knowledge is defined in the 21$^{st}$ Century. Many of the world's most successful business leaders never finished high school and/or college. These individuals lived out their talents through their own actions and determination—attaining the necessary knowledge to succeed before the start of globalization and the information era engrossed the world. Nowadays there is so much information out there; many have come to find that discovering the right answer is not always that simple. The power of knowledge and expertise in one's field is a necessary determinant when deciding who we interact with for relevant services and products from simple research for a paper to our next appliance purchase. We do not just simply ask a random stranger on the street to provide professional medical services; we seek out a licensed doctor or health practitioner who has the medical knowledge necessary to render his or her services.

Information is knowledge and knowledge is the gateway to success. I would define knowledge as one's expertise in a specific field and the ability to transfer that information to a wider audience. Therefore, one should spend time honing his or her talents and skills, learning new experiences, and have a willingness to be a life-long learner. Many folks, as they get older, begin to talk about their regrets in life—from not spending more time with their kids to never finishing college. We will all have regrets; however, there is no reason we should. Living every minute of every day as an opportunity to learn new experiences, to grow in knowledge, and to attain one's dreams is the defining core of the human life that makes us unique beings. The growth of the information age and the expansive treasure-trove of knowledge that is out there enable us all to reach out to those with similar interests, learn from the failure of others, be inspired by the success of others, and to make a lasting positive difference in the world.

Life is filled with many trials and tribulations; it is when we are at our weakest and darkest moments that we pick ourselves up and live out the life that each of us has imagined. The struggle of life itself is one that allows us to constantly reinvent our own individual selves. Each person must decide right from wrong; good and evil; and whether they will seek hope over fear; and opportunity over failure. No one should ever settle for anything other than full and complete opportunity and success. Just like the seasons, knowledge comes and goes with the ages, but one must never negate the opportunity to seek it.

## Find Your Creative Space and Be Inspired

There are so many great and inspiring stories out in the world. Stories about families, friends, communities, schools, businesses, and dreams coming true that has yet to be discovered. The dedication and perseverance of so many people to be inspired by their own ideals and aspirations as well as those of others, is quite fascinating. The goals people have, the lives people create, and ultimately the legacies we all leave to future generations are determined by our abilities to live the life we each have imagined. This life could be inspired by our connections with others, stories, music, and the intricacies and complexities of life itself. What each and every one of us eventually becomes is of our own making—it is the completion of our own destiny. The paths we take may be different, complicated, and filled with mysterious occurrences, but eventually these paths must come to an end one way or another with truth or the lack thereof. Not all of us will reach our destination for a myriad of reasons, but the opportunity and the door is always there waiting to be opened, waiting to be inspired and developed.

The moment we each realize that we are on that path and that our own inspirations are coming to fruition is a quite tantalizing and unique experience. Every person is so very different—the way we think, create, design, and live. My dream is my dream as yours is yours. Our destinies may at some point connect, but at the end of the day we are each our own person. It is quite amazing that many people spend decades imagining and creating their futures while some reach their dreams quickly.

The ability to shape our own destinies is always within grasp of our willingness to take risk and to live in the moment. Inspiration is something that comes and goes for many, as it is the driving force behind success and creativity. People who live out their dreams are constantly inspired by their work and those who support their efforts in their unique life journeys.

We all face our own trials and tribulations; ups and downs; successes and failures; but nothing should hold back an individual from believing in his or her own talents and abilities to change the world. And by world, I do not necessarily mean the whole planet, but your own individual world. We all have that perfect space, that unique sense of pride and creative inspiration that we tap into to keep us going and believing in ourselves. This could be anything, from religion to writing poetry to doing yoga in an open grass field. Wherever your creative and inspiring space is, this is where you attain your motivation and creative juice to be you! Only you can be you and no one else can take your place or your sense of being and reality. We each believe what we believe to be the truth based on our own upbringings, family, friends, life situations, and aspirations. The unique sphere we place ourselves in ultimately determines our present and our future.

Sometimes it is very hard to live the dreams we have always imagined and believed in the face of so much destruction, pain, and suffering we feel as though the cup is always half empty. But, in the midst of the storm, there is a brighter light on the other side that has each and every one of our names on it and holds our dreams and our deepest passions in life. It is our creative fingerprint, our destiny to be inspired and to live inspired every single day. Once we come to the full realization that life is fleeting, that our time here is as short as a morning breeze, we can then take what we have learned, what we believe, what we have imagined, and be inspired to live it! We all have unique talents that can make not only our own lives fulfilled, but those of others around us—helping to shaping the future in the present. Take a leap of faith, explore new horizons, find your creative space, live the life you have imagined, and be inspired to shape a more positive world for others!

## Run Away from the Crowd

There is something comforting about standing in a crowd, because you are not alone. The thought is, "if everyone else is doing it, then it must be the right way" or "why go the opposite direction or really follow my dreams when so many others have succeeded doing this exact thing." Most people live in a "crowd effect" world—where their actions are pre-determined based on what others expect of them or simply what seems to work at the time. It takes hard work and stamina to tap into the creative talents within the individual mind and to truly own your destiny. If the crowd is warm, massive, and standard—why search for a new spot? Why create a new wheel? Why run into the unknown darkness of the world seeking light?

From the day we start grade school we are taught to conform to a core set of standards, from our classroom etiquette and behavior to coloring inside of the lines. We are given hall passes to determine when and if we can use the bathroom, rigid classroom schedules with a core set of courses that are considered "college prepara-tory" or you can settle for the "basic" course load, which really means the school system has no faith in your academic potential. The world has always been developed to separate individuals of all ages, races, and economic backgrounds into "crowds". Depending on the crowd you have been placed in will determine how you fare for the rest of your life—or at least that is the conventional wisdom. Instead of settling into the mundane "crowd effect", many run away from the crowd and seek their own creative isolation. They discover that a world in which people are placed into a crowd system is not exactly how we were born to function. Even if all men are created equal, that does not exactly translate into "all men therefore think alike or look alike or do the same things."

We as humans have a unique and compelling life story of challenging the crowd effect to create something that moves our society forward—that pushes the envelope of ingenuity and breaks down the barriers of close-mindedness. The idea of simply being just another shadow in a crowd should force all who are in a permanent state of complacency to re-evaluate their life and to once again realize his or her God-given abilities. It is amazing how so many people are satisfied with living in a crowd-ed space of similar ideas. There is so much yet to be discovered, created, and devel-oped that is craving for an inventor. When your creative spirit is matched with your love of life, then you know that you are in the right space. Keep believing in yourself, plugging away at your visions, and never give up until you have reached your destina-tion. If you are not working towards your own independence in some way, shape, or form, then you will always be a product of the "crowd effect"—slaving away for another person's success that is not yours and building their creative empire; watch-ing as your own dreams deteriorate into the world of "has-beens" or daily regret of "only ifs".

No one wants to live that life, but ultimately that is where 90% of people end up. How you find yourself in that 10% who decided not to just be another member of the crowd is mostly up to you and your own ability to enact the change and creativity you seek. Finding your passion, sharing it, and honing it takes time, hard work, risks, and a constant focus on your vision that will eventually lead to ultimate happiness and success. Never do something only for the benefit of others; you learn quickly the impossibility of pleasing everyone. Live your life doing what you love and success will surely follow.

### Are You an Idea or a Widget?

The power to shape and mold our own being on this earth is a responsibility that we should all embrace. Determining exactly where we each fit in, how our talents can be used for the improvement of society, and whether or not we will simply be a widget or a sustainable idea, is the calling of this generation. Are you simply an icon or widget for someone else to shape and control, or will you become an idea that lasts for generations and spreads innovation and creativity? This is the question of our time. In order to achieve success you must believe in yourself, you must act and do in your best interests, and most importantly, you must represent an idea that positively changes the lives of people around you. When a powerful and inspiring idea spreads, it can change the world. Just a simple look at the world will show you a place of ideas that were once denied, left behind, pushed to the side, or given up on. However, there was always someone who believed in that idea, fought for it, breathed it, and lived it. These ideas stretched cultures, continents, and oceans. These ideas represented the discovery of medical breakthroughs to modern farming and agriculture, the Internet, and so forth.

Once you discover your purpose and the idea that you shall carry forth, life becomes a mission and has no boundaries. You begin to fully understand and grasp your own unique story and being. Everyone has a compelling purpose, even if they have yet to find it or accept it. Our souls and minds are engineered for greatness, for hope, justice, and prosperity. Even in a world filled with hate, destruction, hopelessness, poverty, and disease, there shall be light at the end of the tunnel. When people decide to not only be mere spectators, but active participants in the game of life, our society as a whole will reap the benefits of a people who stand for something, rather than fall for anything. The story of the human cause is one which that has endured triumph and failure, hope and sorrow, resurrection and death, and the story has not yet ended, it is just beginning. Even as the clock runs out and death takes another soul, birth and the newness of life endure. New life itself is an enduring idea that promises to give meaning and purpose to a new chapter for a new generation that has not yet fully been written.

That is the difference between being an idea and being a widget. Are you in control of your destiny? Are you the author of your story? Have you forsaken the frailties of negativity and hopelessness for a new beginning? Once you have discovered your meaning, your story, and your idea, you must actively engage others to join you in your quest to make a positive difference in the world. Let not your present and future be defined by past mistakes, but instead embrace the uncertainty of the unknown, live life to the fullest, and dream of a future that represents the joy of new life.

## Creating Your Own Idea and Defining Your Life

If you were to flip open a dictionary and there was a definition for every human on this earth, what exactly would be scribbled next to your name? How would you be defined? Would you be defined by your job, interests, achievements, past or present? Discovering your own definition is vital to determining your purpose on earth. How many people do you know who are defined by the work they do or the long hours they put in at the office? When you are defined merely by an inanimate industry or object, it is quite fleeting. Nothing is meant to last forever and as we are slowly recovering from the 'Great Recession' we have all witnessed the dispensability of employment.

Take a step back and look at yourself in the mirror to determine how others define you and what you are defined by. And if those two images clash with how you would like to be defined, then you know it is time for a change. Those who are successful in life are rarely defined by an industry, product, or service—they are defined by an idea. Simply look at those who are regarded as rattlers of the status quo—Mahatma Gandhi, Martin Luther King, Jr., Mother Theresa, Bill Gates, Steve Jobs, and so forth. If Apple was to file for bankruptcy today and Steve Jobs was forced out, his legacy would still live on. There is no doubt in my mind that he would literally be able to start a new company based on the idea of his achievements at Apple the day after, and consumers would rush to join whatever cause he promoted.

People like Gandhi, Martin Luther King, Jr. and Mother Theresa spread an idea of peace and love. That is what they wanted to be defined by, and still today, we see those individuals as shining lights of humanity. There is no doubt that attaining celebrity status, starting a popular business venture and so forth, helps individuals to attain a certain level of authenticity and credibility. People listen and aspire to be those individuals who have become great success stories and who have achieved greatness in their respective fields.

However, at the end of the day everything that is created and that will be created started with an idea. Apple was created based on the idea of a different look and design that PC's were not offering. Wal-Mart was created based on the idea of reducing costs for consumers so they can save more of their own money. Facebook was created on the idea of social networking. Therefore, as individuals we must all discover our talent or idea—that we will define and shape to be our own, instead of them shaping us. We are all truly unique and amazing beings that have the power of the universe at our fingertips. Discover your talents and define your present and future.

## What If?

There are a lot of what ifs that come into our minds that keep us from reaching our full potential. The fear, the doubt, the excuses, the moments of self pity, jealousy, anger, and so on. If we put as much energy in achieving and believing in ourselves that we do in the "what ifs", there will be a lot more successful and happy people in the world. There is always going to be fear and doubt, but to live your true purpose you must reach for the unknown, turn your back on fear and negativity, and live out your destiny. Having faith in your God-given talents and aspirations will inspire others around you to believe in you. People are drawn to energetic, hopeful, and positive energy, so live your life believing before seeing and hoping for what is to come, while at the same time working diligently everyday towards your ultimate goals and dreams.

What if....
People laugh at me?
I fail?
Only 10 people show up?
I only get 3rd place?

I don't get this promotion?

I don't get this job?

No one really cares?

It's too hard? It scares me?

I won't be able to finish?

I'm not the one for the task?

I'll just do it tomorrow or next week or next year?

I'm not talented enough?

No one will listen to me?

My voice doesn't matter?

I'm not smart enough?

*What if I succeed?*

## The Puzzle of Life: Finding the Missing Pieces

The challenges of life are much like a puzzle. We have all had that one puzzle where some of the pieces were missing. We knew exactly what the shapes were and where they would fit in, but we just could not find the pieces. There are times in life where we are in the exact same situation. We know where we want to go, we have the vision, the goals, and the determination, but we are lacking something. A piece is missing to fully succeed at the task at hand. For many it may be the lack of an educational degree or funds or a network to exchange ideas and resumes. However, that is no excuse for anyone to simply quit seeking out those pieces to the puzzle of life. If you know where you want to go and what success looks like, then the quest must be continuous and exceedingly ambitious. We each have a role on this earth and we are each a piece to a larger puzzle. Our individual and group contributions are vital to making the world a better place today and for future generations. Whatever your skills or talents are, they can be put to use right now—today! Everyone has the capacity to live his or her dreams and be an innovator. Do not let others tell you that you cannot live your dreams. Life is all about overcoming the challenges that present themselves and beating the odds. Everything that you see, hear, touch, smell, etc. started out as a simple idea. From the clothes you wear to the doors you open to the book page you are looking at right now. Let not your heart be troubled by war, destruction, and suffering, instead see those cries for help as an opportunity to make life better—not just for yourself, but for the world around you.

At one point or another, we will all be missing pieces to the puzzle of life, but once you find those pieces and your purpose for living, you will see that life is filled with joy, opportunity, and a chance to make a positive difference in the world. Discover your calling and push ahead, and do not just hope for a better tomorrow, create it!

### The Future of Social Networking and Idea Development

We have seen a huge explosion of social networking sites in the last five years or so. Some have lasted, many have disappeared into oblivion. As social networking continues to evolve, a pattern that continues to arise is the creation of niche social sites to further develop the power of the web. For instance, Twitter is a great example of a social niche that truly is for web and information junkies, which probably would not exist without the explosion of Facebook. There are sites like Jumo that seek to partner users with non-profit organizations or Flickr that allows users to digitally share their photos. There are hundreds of niche sites out there that feed off the power of social networking. This will continue to expand over the coming decade and there is no reason to believe there is anything to slow it down. More and more people are seeking out more specific web portals to share ideas, to spread information, to showcase their talents, to seek out potential business partners, and so forth.

Users are craving a way to better express their ideas and passions to the outside world through the utilization of the Internet and the power of social networking. Due to our globally connected society it is much easier to develop a web-based only idea, instead of building a brick and mortar store front. Web-based innovations spread faster, are cheaper to develop and change over time, and provide millions of people in a matter of minutes with the opportunity to explore and take part in something new and interesting.

There is a gap in the universe of what Facebook founder Mark Zuckerberg calls the "social graph", which is the mapping of people and their relationship to one another. The gap that exists is how those relationships are enhanced into a more viable and relevant real-world product and impact. The ability of users to decipher the wealth of information and knowledge that the Internet and social networking provides to actually create a more practical outcome in the real world vs. the virtual world is the next challenge and frontier in the social atmosphere.

Social networking has allowed users to find similar people with the same ideas, goals, and aspirations. This has greatly increased the spreading and sharing of ideas and knowledge between users. However, there is still no central location on the web for ideas and knowledge to be better molded and shaped into viable products or services. The question then becomes, how do we synthesize that wealth of information and knowledge into workable, concrete actions?—essentially moving from the theoretical to the practical.

There are millions of users with potential monumental ideas on a breadth of issues or problems that need to be solved in the form of science, technology, and other innovative fields. To create a web portal for users of the Internet to come together; to better understand their own personalities and how they relate to entrepreneurship; and to develop the opportunity to connect with like-minded creative minds, is the challenge of our generation—to move from simply the realm of ideas to the reality of action and prototypes.

We live in a much more open and dynamic society, where users are more comfortable with sharing and expressing their hopes, dreams, fears, and ideals to a mass amount of people—both strangers and friends. The problems we face as a society are quite large and continuously expanding. To compliment the "social graph", the creation of an "idea graph" would be quite effective in tackling vital social and technological challenges facing the globe. The ability to gather ideas and challenges, then to categorize them, and match them with potential problem solvers, the user, creates an amazing opportunity to promote and empower sustainable social change and innovation.

The resources, knowledge, and users are already out there, thanks to social networking. Creative minds must come together to further expand the ability of social networking to have an increasingly positive and influential impact on making the world a better place through innovation.

## What Are You Waiting For?

What is holding you back from starting your dream, living your destiny, making tomorrow your vision of the future, living for something greater than yourself and creating your art? Everything around you is a potential inspiration to create something great and empowering. Start simple.

1)  Write down the steps you need to take to live your dream.
2)  Who can help you get there?
3)  Determine the resources you will need to succeed.

4) Create a time line with measurable goals that are realistic.

5) Determine your vision and how you plan to get there.

6) What are the costs?

7) And most importantly, write down how you plan to change the world through your art and how it will positively impact other people.

There will always be a hundred excuses to hold off from achieving your goals, naysayers, procrastinators, risks, unforeseen troubles, and roadblocks, but those who achieve their goals in life, that live for a better tomorrow, and that believe in their ability to change the world forge a new path in their quest to be exceptional change agents. There is no reason you cannot do the same. You can unite your senses and awe inspiring abilities to awaken a new narrative in your life and the lives of others. What is your story? How will it begin and end? What is the climax? Who are the characters? What is the plot? You must chart your life and believe—even when you cannot always see over the other side of the valley. Stay vigilant, positive, and never give up. Share your goals and visions with friends, family, strangers, and anyone else who is willing to listen. Live in a way that inspires others to spread ideas that empower even more people.

## Manifest Your Own Destiny

Once you have allowed yourself to be controlled and essentially a manifested image of your position—your career, or college, or some entity that has nothing to do with your own ideas, your creativity, or your sense of being—then you have sold yourself short. There is truly something amazing about each and every person that is the foundation of our existence. The hopes and dreams, visions of a brighter future, the aspirations for greatness and success—all of these experiences are truly the point of life. The experiences that we create, that we build, that we endure, and that we live are what prepare us for a full life with purpose. What you make of opportunities in life, not necessarily what they make of you, determines your path in life. Being defined by a reality that one cannot control, or shape, or move, causes one to become stagnant in his or her own quest for a full existence and understanding of one's purpose and ability to create real and lasting change.

I have always believed wholeheartedly in the power of one's own innate ideas and creative inspirations to shape one's own world or reality. A reality that only exists if we believe in it, if we fight for it, if we work for it, and if we persevere against all the negative comments and negative energy that seeks to tear down and destroy, rather than lift up and sustain. The human cause is unyielding, it is deep, and it is monumental. The ability to reach across the sky, to stretch across new borders and opportunities is the catalyst for becoming awakened to one's own passions and love of life. Once you are able to realize that you have a purpose, that you are worthy of a successful and happy life without regard to what others think, or a position or some other stigma that you cannot control, then doors will open and your life path will be enlightened.

The energy that each person puts out in the world is what he or she will get in return. Your treatment of other people, your faith, your determination, and spirit of diversity are paramount to realizing your true potential and living it. When you can be fearless in the face of adversity, free in times of strife and struggle, hopeful even when darkness overshadows the light and always leaning forward, thinking of new creations, designing your own life map, and knowing that you can control your thoughts, your ideas, your life, and ultimately your destiny—this is when you know you are on the path to living your destiny. And once you can take hold of that image of living freely and without fear to knock down doors, to break through barriers, to brainstorm your dreams into reality—you will gain a new sense of purpose and identity that is always focused on being the best you can be by setting priorities, goals, and endeavors to live a life worth dreaming, your destiny will be directly connected with your own freedom to live and inspire. Do not be afraid of the peanut gallery, the nay-sayers, the pretentious, or those who seek to tear down—instead take that negative energy and shape it into a positive force for good.

You know you are making positive strides when the voices of negativity are growing louder, because they want you to fail, they want you to live a mediocre life, and they want you to settle for less. That is when you know that you must endure, that your journey is not in vain, and that your life has purpose and meaning. Live freely, share, love, cry, trek, breathe, run, speak, sing, dance, create, build, reconstruct, whistle, design, fall down, get back up, draw, and most importantly, be you!

### Spreading Our Gifts

It is much easier to hide our gifts than it is to express them. We fear humiliation, failure, negativity, and the nay-sayers. We allow fear to control our emotions and creative forces. Instead we should be governed by the art of humanity and each of our unique abilities to empower those around us. Each of our gifts to positively and consequentially change the world for the better is a calling that we are each expected to uphold. There are times when we may doubt our gifts—fearful of the potential success that our hard work and dedication will bring us. We succumb to the status quo, we fear allowing what is on the inside to shine on the outside, but why? Because human nature or at least the way society has brainwashed us, tells us to follow the safe path—the risk-free order of life—and to not explore our own innermost passions and goals. We choose to allow others to live our dreams, while we simply stand on the sideline waiting for our turn that will not come unless we aim for it.

However, in order to live a truly fruitful life and to impact the world around us, we must go against the grain and the way things are, and beat back the wave that is holding us back from creating and shipping our ideas to the rest of society. Living and shipping your gifts is not just about sharing them with yourself or a few friends, it is about sharing your gifts to the unknown, to a world craving for energetic and idealistic inspirations and breaking down barriers that are keeping you from living your destiny. Constantly moving forward, living your dreams, empowering others, and taking a journey into the unknown—this is the calling of life, this is the purpose of humanity and a society that can only survive based on the best of our intentions. Let your mind be free, let your gifts and ideas spread in the wind, and ultimately the universe will rejoice in your newfound courage, optimism, and success.

## What Money Can't Buy: Social Progress

When you think of the happiest and most exciting times of your life, what do they typically revolve around? Family, friends, personal experiences, trips, community service, creative entrepreneurial adventures, and very altruistic activities are just a few that come to mind. A perfect example of an experience that money could never buy was my time in City Year in Washington, DC, a national non-profit organization aimed at reducing the dropout rate in America and empowering young people. I was practically living off less than $200 a month from the small stipend we received after paying rent and other bills. Luckily, as a member of AmeriCorps I was eligible for food stamps, along with most of my fellow corps members. Living with three other corps (Dave, David, and Hal) members in a two bed-room apartment outside of Washington, DC was quite the experience.

I learned how to spend wisely, to enjoy the little things in life, to find a deeper meaning in life through the work that I was doing and the children I was attempting to positively impact. I was quite happy with my friends and generally the experience of the City Year program. It was something that money could have never bought. The idea of giving time and a piece of the human soul to others who are striving and reaching for something greater in life than their present circumstances allow, is a truly inspiring gift to give to another. And it does not require wealth or connections or any egotistical value; instead it requires a heart, a sense of community, and a belief that all people are created equal and deserve to live in a land of opportunity that tears down barriers, instead of building them.

Money cannot buy true passion for living, it cannot bring out your creative juices, and it cannot give you eternal fulfillment. Sure, money can create momentary joy, it can be a great tool to invest in a new business or to help those less fortunate. However, in order to create a sustainable and well-nurtured society much more has to be done not just in terms of financial investment, but also how we teach our kids from day one, how institutions are structured, how systems work, and what we as a nation can do to ensure education, business development, urban reform, clean energy development, and more include all people and spreading ideas that last and can be transferred from community to community. We all have an obligation to fight for social progress, to fight for human rights, and the virtue of humanity.

We cannot turn our backs on the failures of our society as if money will eventually solve all of our problems—simply throwing more money at the black hole of bureaucracy is both naive and unrealistic. We need more creativity, more idealism, and more opportunity for people who are disadvantaged. The more we do to improve our societal mores, specifically how we treat those who are less off, the better off we will be as a nation and a diverse people. The answers to complex problems are always here, waiting to be solved. We all have to spend more time being curious again and breaking out of the structured, rudimentary mindset that for so long most of us have had ingrained into our daily mindset. It is OK to risk failure, to reach for your dreams, to chart a new path, to leap before seeing, and ultimately to have faith in your own destiny to improve society and open new doors for new generations.

## The Slog to Success

Success can be a slog, a turtle race vs. the speed of time with ups and downs, spurts of inspiration, and times of doubt, frustration, and long nights. Many times we end up asking: is it worth it? The simple answer is Yes.

Getting to that point of achieving your goals and living your dreams is the accomplishment we all seek in our lives. There is no better feeling than knowing through hard work, dedication, and the will to succeed (and a little luck) that we beat the odds, the naysayers, and the doubters.

Success can be very slow. We all want that magic Jeannie bottle to make all of our dreams appear in an instant. However, there is something about fighting for your goals, breathing them every second of everyday, and living them to the fullest that makes us who we are. Do not be afraid to step out on faith, take some risks, and put your heart into the ideas and hopes that you believe in. In order to be great you must yearn for it and never cease reaching for something greater than yourself. Your purpose is a fact of destiny; your being here is not a mistake; your life has meaning. You must be unwavering and tenacious in your quest for achievement.

Keep believing in and meditating on your goals, guard them with your heart and mind. Stay focused and unwavering. Wake up knowing that every day is your day to shine, and know that success is not just about enriching your bank account or attending flashy receptions, it is about leaving a positive mark on society. It is about changing the way systems work, helping those less fortunate, and leaving behind an earth that is just a little better than when you got here. Be an inspiration for someone else and live life striving to promote sustainable and lasting social change.

## Standard is Only Good Enough for Our Kids

Have you ever thought about how standard is only good enough for our kids? We give them a standard education with standardized tests, standard text books—typically used from year to year, somewhat standard teachers in most schools, and frankly we only motivate them to achieve standard results. Some kids get picked to attend college, while others get picked to perform "manual labor" for a living, like putting doors on a car in a factory or washing dishes in the back of a restaurant. Do not get me wrong, we need people to perform simple tasks; however, they should at least have a choice to decide. And every person at a young age should at least get an opportunity to choose a more fulfilling and creative life path. Ultimately many will fail, few will succeed, but that is not to say that those individuals who failed did not have the potential to be great or successful. Everyone is born with a special gift or talent. The question is why our society is only providing sub-par resources to our kids, essentially leaving them blinded to the fact that we have failed them for many decades.

As adults, we want the best cars, the best homes, the best and coolest new technologies, the newest shoes, the best jobs and so forth, and most Americans go in debt just to achieve those things in hopes of a paradise of happiness. However, they soon find that sense of happiness was short-lived and then they hit the repeat button over and over again. Then when you look at our education system you see run down school buildings, old text books, ill-prepared teachers, bad school leaders, and a system built for 20th Century learning where the only challenge to students is to do exceptionally well on standardized tests that essentially measure the basic requirements necessary in our society to pass fifth grade, which leaves one wondering how we all got so wrapped up in the idea of a "standard" test? Why not create an "extraordinary" or "exceptional" test? My guess is that our schools are built for standard teaching which typically creates standard results. If our schools taught exceptionally or extraordinarily well, then we would have an extraordinary, exceptional test to measure how great and innovative our students are. Most importantly, we may not need a test at all. We could simply look at how many students were achieving their goals, attending class, staying out of trouble, graduating, starting businesses, and living happy lives.

Teaching students to be basic, to be factory workers, to follow the masses, and to love the status quo cannot be good for America's competitive future in a global economy. We should be teaching our students to be different, to set really big goals, to follow their passions, and to solve, create, and design. And until we do that, our students will continue to be duped, blindfolded, beaten, lied to, and forever destined for a standard way of living and achieving.

### Reaching the Promised Land and Living for a Better Tomorrow

When has the future ever been darker than our past or present? There is always something to hope for and fight for that eludes our current state of being. There are always problems to be solved, bridges to be built, and dreams to be lived. Life is a complicated, untold, daring, and enduring act of courage and sacrifice. Life is about believing before seeing, creating before knowing, and dreaming of a future life that is not yet present. Life is beautiful, colorful, different, messy, risky, scary, hopeful, and ongoing. Living in just the present fails to acknowledge the battles, triumphs, failures, marches, protests, cries, and wars that have gotten us to where we are today. Our own denial of what "can" and "should" be complicates our own ability to live not only in the present, but the future. For far too many people, life is only the here and now, the fears of the present, the guilt of the past, the heartaches from failure, and the trials and tribulations that slowly degrade the inner most being of life and happiness. Instead, life should be an ever growing journey for a brighter tomorrow. Life is a narrative or story that is not to be written by the mind and ideas of another person, but it is to be lived by each individual. Our individual hopes and dreams, ideals, and aspirations can only come forth when we each realize our purpose. We each must be willing to take untold risks in the dark of night, even when our own fears hold us back. To truly live is when life has purpose, meaning, and opportunity. Creating a tomorrow that embraces the hopes and dreams of a new generation is the enduring quest for humanity and social change. Even in our present circumstances, whatever those may be, the time is always ripe to seek a new beginning, to open new doors, and to forge ahead knowing that life has a purpose and that you are an integral part in defining and utilizing your own unique abilities to make a positive difference in the world.

No day is promised, as the future holds our destiny; however, only you can discover and develop that destiny. It is up to you to make the decision on whether or not you shall seek a future based on humanity, prosperity, innovation, creativity, and a calling to make the world a better place. Let not your fear of the unknown hold you back, instead embrace those fears, live them, and conquer them. Only then will you reach the Promised Land.

## The Ask

What effect can you cause? How can your talents be used to change the world? That is the challenge of our generation. Spend some time to develop your goals, to chart a path that improves society in some way, and to live your dreams. This world is craving for young people, this generation, to rise up for something greater than us; to seek peace over war; love over hate; and an enduring belief in the power of many to come together for the greater good. There will be challenges along the way, bumps and bruises; successes and failures, but nothing can stop the flow of a destiny lived. Young people across the world from Egypt to Tunisia are rising up demanding freedom and the ability to simply live their lives. Many of us are already capable of doing just that. The resources are available, the ideas are there—the only thing that is missing is the drive to commit and act. Let us push forward for a brighter future, not just for this generation, but for the next.

# About The Author

The youngest of eight children, Joshua Murphy began his writing career at a very young age even before publishing his first book *Writings from a Teenage Mind* in high school. After writing his own column in a local newspaper for over a year, he attended the University of Tampa attaining a BA in government and world affairs in 2008. During his college years he was actively involved in numerous campus leadership organizations and volunteer projects in New Orleans and Mississippi after Hurricane Katrina. His experiences in college led him to join City Year, a national non-profit aimed at reducing the national dropout rate, where he tutored, taught, and mentored students. Murphy has always been inspired by the power of young people and their ability to enact sustainable social change. Through his writings he hopes to empower and educate people of all ages on how to tap their own creative abilities to make a positive difference in the world. He currently resides in the Washington, DC area and is the Founder and CEO of IDEASLive Media Group.

9920979R0

Made in the USA
Lexington, KY
08 June 2011